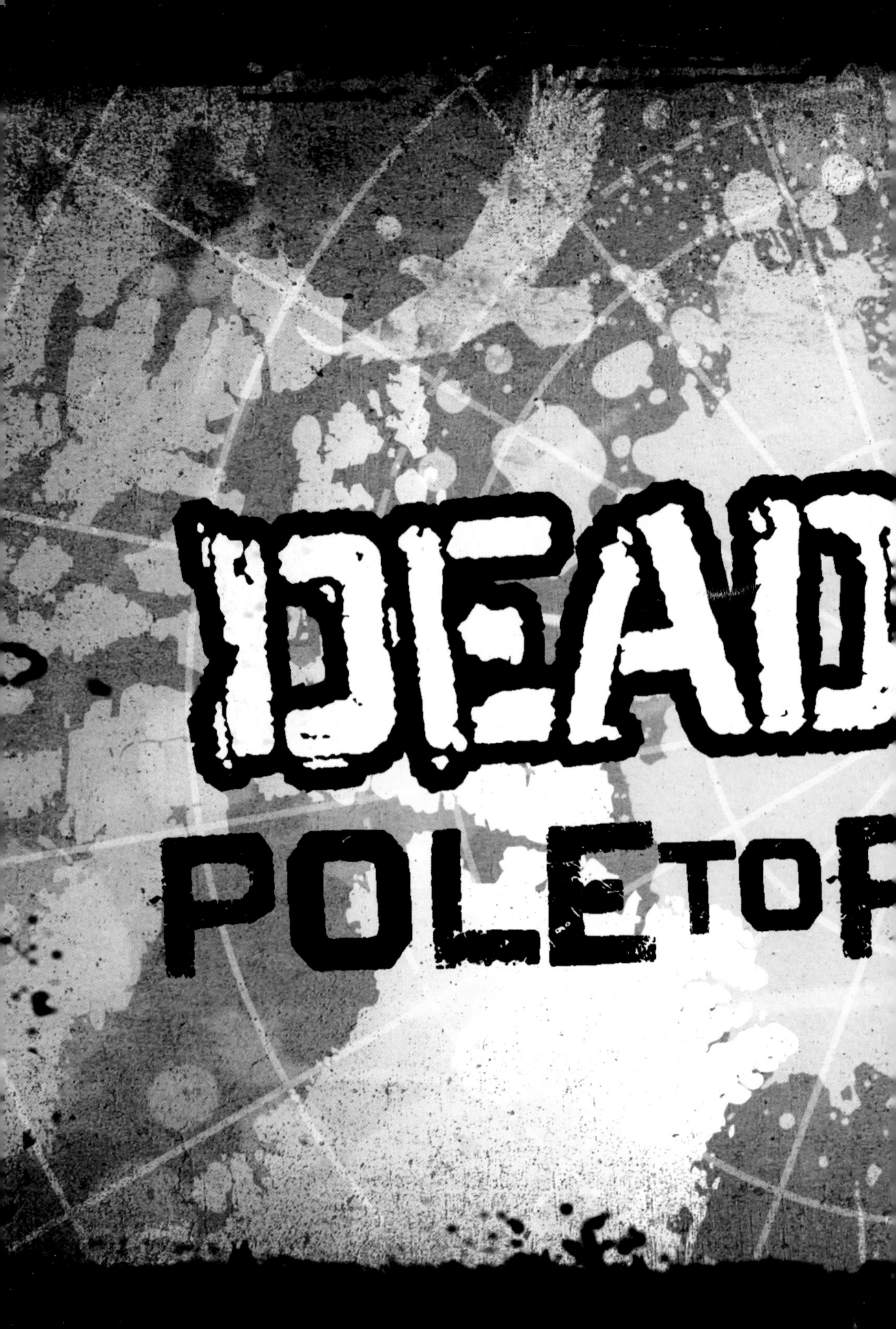
DEAD
POLETOP

Dedicated to the Deadly team,
who worked so hard to make this
dream a reality.
SB

STEVE BACKSHALL

DEADLY POLE TO POLE

Orion
Children's Books

First Published in Great Britain in 2014
By Orion Children's Books
This paperback edition first published in Great Britain in 2015
by Orion Children's Books
an imprint of Hachette Children's Group
and published by Hodder and Stoughton
Orion House
5 Upper St Martin's Lane
London WC2H 9EA
An Hachette UK Company

1 3 5 7 9 10 8 6 4 2

Text copyright © Steve Backshall 2014
Derived from and based on the BBC TV series *Deadly Pole to Pole*.

A catalogue record for this book is available from the British Library.

ISBN: 978 1 4440 1559 1

Printed and bound in China

MIX
Paper from
responsible sources
FSC® C008047

www.orionchildrensbooks.co.uk

The Pole to Pole team was only able to visit and explore locations and observe animal
species after many months of research and consultation with scientists, specialists and
safety professionals and only after comprehensive risk assessments had been made.
Readers should not attempt to replicate activities in this book without professional
advice and assistance.

CONTENTS

SOMERSET ISLAND

SVALBARD

ALASKA

BRITISH COLUMBIA   YELLOWSTONE

CALIFORNIA   TEXAS

HAWAII   CUBA   BAHAMAS

MEXICO   GUYANA

BRAZIL

PATAGONIA

FALKLANDS   SOUTH GEORGIA

ANTARCTIC PENINSULA

DEADLY CHALLENGE

After six years of making Deadly 60, the crew and I had ticked off a lifetime of wild wonders. We had been to all but one continent, and I'd visited 104 countries. We'd filmed thousands of animals, many of which are endangered, or had never been seen on screen before. We'd been hunted by Komodo dragons, measured the bite of six species of crocodile, shared the seas with more than twenty species of shark, caught the most poisonous and most venomous creatures known to science, soared with eagles and free-dived alongside the largest animal that has ever lived. I'd also been bitten, on camera, by a crocodile and an anaconda, and stung by an assortment of scorpions, wasps and other beasts. It was kind of difficult to know what to do next. Deadly needed a new, bigger challenge.

Scorpion!

My background is in expeditions and the most treasured moments of my life have always been in the wildest and most remote corners of our planet. My new plan was to turn Deadly into one huge expedition, and to journey to parts of the world I had yet to explore. So what to choose? Big mountain ranges were out – there are not enough animals living there to make a whole series. I didn't want to traverse the planet at the equator, because the whole trip would be in tropical heat and it would have started to feel all the same. The obvious answer was to travel right around the globe, from Pole to Pole. Travelling through the latitudes north to south, we would start in polar ice, with icebergs, polar bears and pack ice, then journey across Arctic tundra, temperate forests and oceans, passing through the tropic of Cancer to deserts, tropical forests, coral reefs, wetlands and swamps, then crossing the equator, before going through the tropic of Capricorn. As we continued south we would once again break out into chilly tundra, glaciers, icebergs and the Antarctic ice cap.

Every environment we explored would have different animals and challenges. It would be the most diverse wildlife journey ever filmed.

Originally I wanted the journey to start and end at the Poles themselves. However, the brutal truth is that there are no animals living at either Pole. We would have wasted time slogging to places where nothing lives, and ultimately, Deadly is all about wildlife. The sensible compromise was to start way up in the Arctic Circle in Svalbard, and finish at the

Some of our luggage on the dock at the Falkland Islands.

Antarctic Peninsula, both of which provide an overdose of wild wonders. The journey would take over a year and meant I would be away from home, family and friends for many months at a time, but it would be the greatest of all adventures.

The team clustered round maps, measured distances with intensely concentrated faces, made phone calls to far-flung places and did their best to convince incredulous health and safety people that what we were suggesting was possible to achieve without anyone getting eaten. They worked incredibly hard for many months and finally on 5 January 2013, five of us turned up at Heathrow airport, bubbling with excitement and ready for the adventure of a lifetime.

Steve

Lena
Aldan
VERKHOYANSKIY
KHREBET
Okhotsk
Sea of
Okhotsk
Oymyakon
GORACHEN 10217 FT
CHERSKOGO
KHR
KHREBET
Seymchan
Verkhoyansk
Yana
Indigirka
Verkhne-Kolymsk
Kolyma
Magadan
Bukun
Nordvik
POLUOSTROV
MYS CHELYUSKIN
OSTROV KOTELNY
More Laptevykh
NOVO-SIBIRSKIYE OSTROVA
Krestyakh
Vostochno
Sibirskoye More
POLUOSTROV
KAMCHATKA
KHREBET
Gulf of Gizhiginsk
Gizhiga
GYDAN
Omolon
Ambarchik
Nizhne-Kolymsk
OSTROV AYON
KORYAKSKIY
KHREBET
OSTROV KARAGINSKIY
Markovo
Anadyr
ANADYRSKIY KHR
7512 FT
16848 FT
OSTROV VRANGELYA
Chukchee
Sea
KOMANDORSKIYE OSTROVA
MYS OLYUTORSKIY
US-RUSSIA CONVENTION OF 1867
Anadyrskiy Zaliv
Bering
Strait
DIOMEDE IS
Barrow
PT BARROW
Beaufort Sea
BROOKS RANGE
SEWARD PENINSULA
Norton Sound
Nome
Yukon
Tanana R
ALASKA
Bethel
ALASKA RA
Anchorage
Fairbanks
ALEUTIAN ISLANDS
Bering

DEADLY POLE TO POLE

THE ARCTIC

We started our journey in the Arctic, an incredibly remote land where conditions can be brutal. This is the area at the far north of our planet and is defined by the Arctic Circle, the line of latitude at 66.6 degrees north of the equator. It includes the Arctic Ocean, much of which is covered by ice, and the northern parts of Scandinavia, Russia, Canada, Greenland and Alaska. In winter, the area of sea ice on the Arctic increases greatly and temperatures can fall as low as –68 degrees centigrade.

SVALBARD

Our epic expedition began far up in the Arctic Circle, in the Svalbard archipelago. At latitude 81 degrees north, it is just a metaphorical stone's throw from the North Pole itself. We chose Svalbard as our starting point because it is the best place in the Arctic for Deadly wildlife. There are more polar bears here than people!

The *Havsel*, our Arctic home.

Our home for the first eight days of our journey was the *Havsel*, a rusty icebreaker, with several cosy cabins where we could escape the bitter chill and crashing waves. It's easily the biggest vessel we've ever had to ourselves in all the years of filming Deadly, but we needed it. It was summer in the far north and there was sunlight for twenty-four hours a day, but towards the Pole there was still dense pack ice and huge icebergs that would sink anything other than an icebreaker. The *Havsel*, however, could thunder her 400 tonnes through pack ice and even take on a decent-sized iceberg. Just as well, as the idea of sinking in waters this cold and trying to survive doesn't bear thinking about.

Greedy gulls

Our main focus was of course the polar bear, great icon of the northern wilds, but there were plenty of other target animals. After a night's steam from Longyearbyen, the Svalbard capital, we pitched up at some forbidding-looking sea cliffs. Circling overhead were scores of birds, in numbers so great that they appeared more like a vast swarm of bees. By far the most numerous were little auks, the most common seabird in the Arctic. There were hundreds of thousands, perhaps millions of them. We headed to the slopes where they were nesting. In among the rocks were nooks and crannies, and deep within you could hear the chicks making strange churring noises, a little like penguin chicks.

Above: Flocks of little auks and guillemots.
Following pages: Filming seabirds from our boat, the *Havsel*, near Svalbard.

The auks themselves careered past us, using their flocking behaviour to protect them from predators, the most obvious of which were glaucous gulls. These large grey-winged seabirds snatch the little auks on the wing, grabbing their legs and yanking them out of the sky. This is made all the easier for the gulls because the auks are heavy, with full crops (a crop is a pouch near the throat for food storage), having collected huge amounts of krill to feed to their youngsters. It was a long, freezing cold day out on the cliffs.

The wind was extreme, and at some moments we had to lean into it just to stay standing while we watched the birds!

Arctic heavyweights

Back at sea, we steamed for twenty-four hours to our next destination. Already our body clocks had been completely thrown by the constant daylight. We would sleep most of the day and then wake in the middle of the night to film. Two humpback whales popped up alongside the boat, and we jumped up and out to film them feeding, half of the crew still in their pyjamas despite the sub-zero temperatures!

One of the highlights of the trip for me was spotting a true Arctic specialist – the walrus. An adult male walrus can be nearly two tonnes in weight, with teeth or tusks measuring as much as a metre long. The walrus is the third largest pinniped (pinnipeds are the group of mammals to which seals, sea lions and walrus belong) after the humungous northern and southern elephant seals.

Steve kayaking with walrus in Svalbard.

Walrus are spooked by motorised boats, so I approached in a kayak. The walrus were immediately curious, but came towards me perhaps ten at a time, keeping the safety of numbers. With each one weighing as much as a family estate car and able to cheerfully splinter my kayak into little plastic matchsticks, this was pretty heart-in-mouth stuff.

One walrus popped up so close alongside me that I couldn't even put my paddle into the water to move away without hitting him in the face! A couple of others got so bold that they looked as if they were about to put one of their massive tusks

through the back of my kayak. Soon we decided that discretion should be the better part of valour, and headed back to the big boat – me with my heart pounding in my chest. Deadly Pole to Pole had well and truly begun!

> ## PORTRAIT OF A PREDATOR
> ### WALRUS (Odobenus rosmarus)
> **Maximum size:**
> 1,700 kilograms; 3.5 metres long.
> **Range:**
> Canadian Arctic, Greenland, Russia, with both North Atlantic and North Pacific sub-species.
> **Deadly facts:**
> walrus dive to the seabed and suck clams out of their shells, using the vacuum action from their rubbery lips. Tusks can be 1 metre long.

The walrus come close.

A polar bear climbing the near-vertical cliff.

The ice bear

The last word though inevitably goes to the polar bear. On average, it is the largest land carnivore, although bigger individual grizzly bears from Kodiak Island in Alaska have been known. The polar bear is also one of the only animals on Earth that will on occasion deliberately hunt and eat a human being, so we needed to be vigilant.

Perhaps our most jaw-dropping encounter was at the bird cliffs. As we arrived, there was a big white head

PORTRAIT OF A PREDATOR

POLAR BEAR *(Ursus maritimus)*

Maximum size:

600 kilograms; 2.6 metres long.

Range:

across the Arctic North,

on or near sea ice.

Deadly facts:

can swim 100 kilometres plus in a day. The hairs of a polar bear are hollow and not coloured – white light reflects around inside them giving them their classic hue.

bobbing through the sea underneath the rock. As we watched in disbelief, the polar bear swam to the rockface, and clambered up the near-vertical cliffs. At one point, he came to a couloir (a gully in the rock) that was filled with packed ice. The bear didn't even flinch, but just used his long claws as crampons and clambered straight up. He even made a bridging move that was exactly like a highly skilled human climber would do. Presumably the bear was risking his life in order to feast on the birds and their chicks and eggs. It seems that living here in the Arctic makes you endlessly resourceful.

If this was a vision of wonder, the next encounter was rather more tense. It was close to our most northerly point. Here the pack ice proper began and stretched on like a crumpled white duvet for the several hundred kilometres

Following pages: Steve and the team come close to a polar bear.

to the North Pole. The bears need this ice to survive, as they hunt for seals that have hauled out to rest on the frozen floes. They are masters of ambush, preparing their attacks from the water or on the ice, but will creep or swim as close as they possibly can, using their white camouflage to blend perfectly with their surroundings. Then, at the last second they launch an all-out power play, lunging at their prey from short range. They can kill a seal with a single cuff of a mighty paw and will even kill whales that have come to open holes in the ice to breathe. Their strength is extraordinary.

CLOSE SHAVE

It's about two in the morning. I'm lying in my bunk trying to sleep, with my pillow wrapped round my head to blank out the constant sunlight, when I hear the spotters shouting from above, 'Bear, bear, there, in the water!' Our polar bear is swimming through the leads between the ice, steady, committed, keeping a dead straight line and constant pace. Bear in this frame of mind can swim nearly a hundred kilometres without stopping, even in waters that may be below freezing point (the salt means sea water may not freeze until it is minus two degrees). We don't want to distract him from his purpose and can't steer in among the ice in the *Havsel* without attracting his attention, so I clamber down the deck ladder and slide into my sea kayak.

I paddle out with the icebergs bobbing around me, ghostly against the soft pink and powder blue of the sky. My plan is to glide into position ahead of where the bear is swimming, anticipating where he might go so that I can get shots of him in the water. Cameraman Graham has the super-long lens focused on me from the deck of the boat, but by now he is a good kilometre away. I feel very alone,

out here among the icebergs with my bear
swimming towards me.

But something unexpected is happening. I'd put
myself in a position where the bear would cruise a
hundred metres or so in front of me. However, now
he is a good deal closer, his attitude and behaviour is
changing. He's slowing down and swimming behind a berg.
He has climbed partially out of the water and is standing
as tall as he can to get a good look at me. Now he has
slipped back into the water and disappeared. All of a sudden
he's trying to approach from behind me, putting the ice
between us so I can't see him. For a second he appears again,
then dives under the water and out of sight. I stop dead
and feel my blood chill.

There is little doubt in my mind, he's hunting me
and he's very close.

When the bear surfaces again, he's slightly
behind me and nearer still. He swims along nonchalantly,
until he is at his closest to the back of my boat, perhaps
four metres away. Then he makes three or four big powerful
swimming strokes straight towards me, gaining on me
remarkably quickly. Luckily I have my eye on him and
pull hard with my paddles, getting out of his reach.
I'm pretty sure he knows that I've seen him, and thus
his move wasn't fully committed. Even so, my brush
with a polar giant, and icon of the Frozen North
is one I will certainly not forget!

SOMERSET ISLAND

Our next stop was a town called Yellowknife in the far north of Canada, where we waited for a flight to Somerset Island way up in the Arctic Circle. It felt decidedly weird, as in Svalbard, to see blazing sunshine in the middle of the night. Though we had clear blue skies in Yellowknife, there was thick fog 2,000 kilometres north at our destination, so our flight was cancelled.

White whales

When we finally arrived at Somerset Island there was bad news. Summer had come late and the place was still frozen solid with sea ice that

should have melted the previous month. You could drive a truck over it. We had been hoping to film beluga whales in the bay but they would not be able to get in there until the ice was gone and it looked as if it would take months for it to melt away – disaster for our schedule.

We tramped out to the peninsula every day, checking on the progress of the ice. Slowly, slowly, day by day, it started to dissipate. Meanwhile, we killed time by heading

Steve laden with equipment on Somerset Island.

out to film musk oxen and Arctic fox, haring around the island the only way possible, on ATVs – all terrain vehicles. They're a great way of getting around on difficult, rugged terrain, but awful for watching wildlife – way too noisy! One day, we drove down a ridgeline and spotted a herd of musk oxen from about three kilometres away. One of the ATVs backfired like a gun going off and the oxen stampeded into the distance, and just kept on sprinting.

Day four. We were still trapped at Somerset Island and everyone was feeling very frustrated, not to mention tired. In the land of the midnight sun, and constant daylight, you can't get to sleep cos your body is telling you that it's the middle of the day, when it's actually 2am! The real reason for our nerves though was that the beluga whales were still nowhere to be seen. I took a kayak and tried to paddle through the ice floes, but reached a brick wall.

Out on the pack ice.

Well, an ice wall anyway. After trying to tow the kayak over the frozen ground I decided it was too dangerous and headed back to land.

Day six. The ice started to move and someone spotted a distant whale spout through the telescope. Johnny, Nick and researcher Luke were by now getting very good at table tennis, as nobody could get to sleep and there was a table in the main tent.

Day seven. The whales are here! Belugas are the white whales of the Arctic. There are two other species that also live their whole lives in the Arctic Ocean: the bowhead and the narwhal. Belugas though are unmistakable, with their all-white bodies, flexible necks that allow them to look over their shoulders, and big smiles! Most large aggregations of animals come together either for breeding or feeding, but belugas come into this bay to moult. They scrub their bodies on the gravelly bottom, grinding off big chunks of dead skin, seeming to revel in it. Also, as the fresh water pouring into the bay means the temperature is just above freezing, it must feel positively warm to the belugas. Essentially, they use the bay like a beauty salon!

With the shots of belugas in the bag, the crew was desperate to get out of Somerset Island and back on the road south. Unfortunately, hurricane-force winds and blizzards were whipping through the Arctic islands. The plane couldn't land, leaving us stranded. I desperately needed to

PORTRAIT OF A PREDATOR

BELUGA WHALE

(Delphinapterus leucas)

Maximum size:

1,500 kilograms; 5.5 metres long.

Range:

cold Arctic waters.

Deadly fact:

the beluga has a layer of blubber up to 15 centimetres thick to keep out the Arctic cold.

Belugas in the bay.

get south to continue the expedition, and back in the UK office, the team were frantically chasing around trying to reorganise things so that the tight schedule could continue as planned.

By day ten, we'd been tent-bound for three days, getting really bored, eating our way through our supplies and reading a lot of books. Finally the plane was able to reach us and whisked us away south. We were three days behind schedule, which was going to play havoc with the rest of the expedition – and things had only just started.

ALASKA
UNITED STATES

Bethel

Nome

Seward
Strait

Prudhoe
Bay

Beaufort
Sea

Banks
Island

Victoria
Island

Fairbanks

Inuvik

Cambridge Bay

Anchorage

Valdez

Gulf of
Alaska

TRENCH

Dawson

Arctic

Great Bear
Lake

Whitehorse

Great Slave
Lake

Juneau

Fort
Nelson

Lake
Athabasca

Prince
George

Fort
McMurray

Edmonton

THE TEMPERATE NORTH

Baffin Bay
Ilulissat
(Jakobshavn)
Resolute
Pond
Inlet
Sisimiut
(Holsteinsborg)
Nuuk
(Godthåb)
Baffin
Island
Davis
Strait
Gjoa
Haven
Iqaluit
Rankin
Inlet
Arviat
Moncton
Ottawa
Washington, D.C.

From the Arctic we travelled to Alaska, a spectacular land of ice, forest and mountains in the far northwest of North America. Much is wilderness and the climate is harsh, but more than 730,000 people live there – as well as some fantastic wildlife. Our journey continued in British Columbia where we visited Vancouver Island, encountering sixgill sharks and bald eagles, then on to one of the world's most magnificent national parks: Yellowstone, where wolves and bison roam.

ALASKA

Alaska is the biggest state in the US, and the wildest. You can fly for many hours and see nothing below you but mountains, forests, lakes and rivers. For lovers of the wild world, this is the great frontier. Alaska is as diverse as any continent: the north shore is barren, frozen Arctic tundra, the heartland soaring mountains (including Denali, at 6,194 metres the highest on the continent) while in the south are damp temperate forests of sitka spruce, where moose and bear roam. It has eight national parks, including North America's biggest, Wrangell-St Elias, which is nearly half the size of England. Alaska is a place where you can get lost in a forever of wilderness, where a strong person can be seized by madness of solitude, where you can suddenly realise you are not at the top of the food chain. It is also my favourite place on the continent by miles.

Grizzly fishermen

Upon arrival in the small capital of Juneau, we boarded a float-plane or flying boat heading for enormous Admiralty Island. These planes date back to the 1940s, which is good for those who are nostalgic but slightly freaky for anyone who's scared of flying! The plane banked and weaved between the mountains

Float-plane to take us in search of bears.

Above: Grizzly mother and cubs.

Right and following pages: Grizzlies hunting for salmon.

and bays as it searched for a way around the banks of clouds. Finally our pilot found a route through the mist and we dropped down to Pack Creek, where grizzly bear are known to hunt regularly. The plane splashed down, and we waded ashore in leaky welly boots. We walked around the shoreline and noticed our first huge grizzly footprints in the mud.

As soon as we got to the river, there were our first bears. Two subadults (around four years old – they'd left their mother, but were not yet ready to breed) were play-fighting in the shallows. A mother and her two cubs were also there, but giving them a wide berth – perhaps she feared they would attack her youngsters. Certainly the biggest threat to a bear cub's safety is a mature male, who may kill it. Later in the day we hiked into the interior of the island to a shallow place in the river, where salmon rest on their journey upriver to spawn. Over the course of several hours, we saw five more bears,

PORTRAIT OF A PREDATOR

BROWN/GRIZZLY BEAR
(*Ursus arctos*)

Maximum size:
680 kilograms; 3 metres long.

Range:
northern North America,
Europe and Asia.

Deadly fact:
brown bears have been
clocked moving at nearly
50 kilometres an hour.

all hunting mere metres away from us. Bear brilliance.

The guts of a glacier

Our next mission was to go in search not of a deadly animal, but of a force that can move mountains: glaciers, rivers of ice that carve through the landscape. Our helicopter flew us up to the Mendenhall glacier, where I'd spent two weeks camping a few years back. I'd had one of my diciest moments on camera there, when my ice axe slipped

On the Mendenhall glacier in Alaska.

The helicopter takes off after leaving us on the glacier.

while I was climbing inside a glacier. I got flushed down through an ice tunnel, coming to rest teetering on a precipice over the abyss. I was lucky to escape with my life.

This time, however, the glacier was not the same place. Glaciers are living things and always changing, growing and – more than ever now due to climate change – shrinking. My aim was to find a feature in the ice called a 'moulin' which is a weakness, where surface water cuts straight down. The water is just above freezing and forms a vicious waterfall.

After setting up a rope system using ice screws, me and cameraman Johnny abseiled down to a gorgeous ice cave, which was a ludicrous sapphire blue, and explored it as far as possible. Unfortunately it soon ran out, so the only

place left to explore was under the waterfall itself. Johnny couldn't follow with the main camera, as the water would have destroyed it. Instead, I put on my special waterproof dry suit, took the camera we usually use for underwater filming, and descended on my own beneath the falls.

CLOSE SHAVE

This is true exploration. No one has ever been here before – apart from anything else, because this moulin will never before have been quite how we found it. On the surface of the glacier we had been sitting in the sunshine, eating chocolate, feeling pretty safe. However, the second I drop under the waterfall just metres away I know I am in a serious survival situation. The water is battering me senseless, the pain in my head is just awful. I've dropped as far as the rope allows me, trying to capture everything on the camera as I go. It is incredibly frightening to be in a tightening blue tube that could collapse at any moment, and thundered on by water that stops your brain and breathing.

I've got as far as the ropes will take me so I'm ready to switch back into climbing mode. But my fingers are so frozen I can't use them and simple rope skills are near impossible. My heart is jumping, and for a moment I'm really scared. If I get trapped here I would probably not last long. Thankfully, I manage to use my crampons to climb up just a little and get back on to the ropes. I climb up through the falls, delighted to see the sunshine and the silhouettes of the crew above me. Back at the surface everyone was unaware of what I'd been through beneath their feet. But that was nothing compared to the pain when the feeling started to come back to my fingers!

Exploring a moulin.

Learning leviathans

The last sequence we were set to film in Alaska was of humpback whales performing a remarkable manouevre called bubble net feeding. This technique involves several whales coming together, swimming beneath shoals of herring while blowing bubbles from their blowholes to form a shimmering curtain that the fish will not swim through. The fish feel trapped, corralled, unaware of the whales circling below, waiting to pounce. Finally, the whales lunge to the surface with gullets billowing, taking in tonnes of water and fish. They press their huge tongues up against the roof of their mouths, driving out the water and trapping the food on the inside of straining plates of baleen, or whalebone. A few years back I was nearly swallowed by whales surging to the surface while I was in my kayak; one of the most spectacular things that has ever happened to me.

We headed out in a motorboat about 160 kilometres from Juneau, before putting to sea in kayaks. The humpback whales were everywhere. At one stage, a whale breached so close that it could easily have landed on us. It was like a vast submarine suddenly leaping out of the water, drenching us. These whales come here for the abundance of food found in Alaskan summer waters, then later head south to breed. There was a possibility we might meet them again in Hawaii later in the expedition.

That night we camped on a deserted beach, with forest-covered mountains on all sides and snow-capped peaks behind them. Sea otters swam past our tents, and there were bear prints everywhere. We took care to prepare all our food a good way down the beach from where we would be sleeping and we put anything edible, and smelly things like toothpaste, into bearproof canisters, so the animals wouldn't be attracted into camp.

Next morning we headed out in kayaks again. Cameraman Johnny was in a double kayak, with guide Corey paddling him from the back. There were

Humpback whales breaching.

Kayaking among the humpback whales

Steller sea lions annoying the humpback whales.

lots of whales, but more interested in us were the hundreds of Steller sea lions, another old friend of Deadly and the largest species of sea lion. They wouldn't leave us alone, mugging the kayaks and leaping into the air to show off to us. We were having a good time, the whales less so. The sea lions wouldn't leave them alone either and were taking great pleasure in jumping all over them, stopping the whales from resting. It was spectacular, but must have been so annoying for the whales!

Mostly the kayaking was great fun, but the tide here can be fierce. At one time it was flowing round the point on an island faster than we could paddle, and we found ourselves being driven backwards. Johnny had to put down the camera and join in the paddling as we hugged close to the rocks and finally got around. All the while, whales were popping up alongside us, dwarfing us with their vast bulk – they can weigh forty tonnes, which is as much as two fire engines.

PORTRAIT OF A PREDATOR

HUMPBACK WHALE
(*Megaptera novaeanglia*)

Maximum size:

40 tonnes; 15 metres long.

Range:

all oceans.

Migration:

travel between polar waters and breeding grounds near the tropics.

Deadly fact:

a humpback's tongue may weigh 2.7 tonnes, as much as a small Asian elephant.

By day three we still hadn't seen any bubble netting. However, everything was made even more exciting by the appearance of a pod of orca which circled the boat, coming no more than a few metres away from us. Wondrous.

BRITISH COLUMBIA

We now journeyed back to Canada, but to a radically different part of this vast country. Canada is the second largest country in the world after Russia, but has more coastline than any other country, with 202,080 kilometres. This is mostly due to the number of huge islands that make up the nation. One of my favourites is Vancouver Island. It is colossal, within a couple of hours of one of Canada's biggest cities, yet with endless miles of wilderness.

It provided one of the finest of all Deadly moments on series two, when orca leapt around my kayak before going off to hunt a Steller sea lion right in front of us. There was a lot to live up to!

Sinister shark

We were to be scuba diving in the bays and inlets to the south of Vancouver Island, in search of weird aquatic assassins. The first and most important was a little known deep sea predator called the sixgill shark – it does indeed have six gill slits, not five like most other sharks. These animals haunt the deepest and darkest parts of our oceans and probably scavenge on whale carcasses that have sunk to the bottom. They will also catch good-sized fish and have even been known to eat each other!

They're spooky-looking creatures, with milky eyes and dark bodies. I'd never seen one before and, knowing that they so rarely come up into shallow

Sixgill shark.

waters where we would be able to dive with them, I came up with a plan. My idea was to build an underwater CCTV camera, which could be in place on the bottom and monitored from the surface. We would put it alongside a crate that was full of chunks of fish and hopefully would attract a shark. We got a techy camera expert to build a system just for us and it worked well, triggering whenever anything swam in front of it. All we needed now was some patience and luck.

Troll of the deep

Having placed the camera on the bottom, we went in search of other marine wonders to film. The first of these was something of a swimming gargoyle. The wolf eel is actually not an eel, but the world's largest species of blenny. It has an elongated body and a massive troll-like head, with long spindly teeth spilling out of its mouth. At the back of the mouth are teeth shaped more like human molars and used for crunching and grinding. This dentition is essential for breaking into their favourite prey, probably the spiniest animal on Earth, the sea urchin. We found our wolf eel lying in a crack under a rocky overhang, with just his big head poking out. I offered him some fish to try to get him to show a little more of himself, but every time he moved forward to take it, a cheeky yellow and black China rockfish would zip in and snatch it from my fingers. Eventually, though, the wolf eel clearly tired of this nonsense and swam out into the open, giving us a good look at his long, lilac body, with its dark purple blotches.

Steve meets a wolf eel.

Flame-haired dragon

Our next underwater oddity was again a new one for me. Nudibranchs are molluscs, like brightly coloured sea slugs. They are found all over the world and come in flamboyant designs but are usually no bigger than my little finger. In Vancouver Island, though, there are truly giant nudibranchs, which can be as long as a standard spoon, come in luminous orange and white, and are covered in dazzling tendrils and tassles. So far, so gorgeous, but they had a surprise in store. Whereas most nudibranchs graze on algae and are so slow you can't see them moving, the giants are predators. They make their way along the bottom until they encounter tube anemones, which look kind of like trees in a Dr Seuss book. They have a tube-like structure that contains the body, while the tip comes out of the top like a feather duster and plucks small bits of food from the water. The nudibranch will creep up on the anemone,

Nudibranchs swimming past our shark bait.

then rear, bringing the front part of the body up off the sea bed, so it looks like a blazing flame-haired dragon. Then the nudibranch dives into the anemone, attempting to feast on the animal inside. It is utterly exquisite.

We had seen so much underwater, but our CCTV camera had registered no trace of a shark. We decided to leave it in place for that night and next day, then come back and spin through the footage to see if anything had swum by. Many hours into the playback, we saw a shape whip past the shot. A shark's tail! Just minutes later, the whole body moved into view. It had swum past late at night and would be long gone by now, so there was no point in us getting our gear on and trying to find it. We had, though, spotted a fleeting glimpse of a shark that few people ever get to see.

Eagle icon

Our last mission on Vancouver Island was to be another television first. Led by resourceful researcher Kiri and determined director Rowan, the Deadly tech team had developed what is known as a time-slice rig. This is essentially a half circle of aluminium, with small cameras attached all the way around it which can fire off simultaneously. If a piece of action can happen right in the 'sweet spot' at the centre of the ring, you can fly around that moment in time, analysing it from a variety of different angles.

Our plan was to try and time-slice a bald eagle snatching a fish from the surface of a small pond, in much the same way as it would when hunting in the wild. To achieve this with a wild bird would take months, and we only had a single day. So we went to a bird of prey centre to test out the tech and were introduced to Manue, a young, keen and at least partially tame bald eagle.

Time-slice rig in operation.

He was incredibly impressive, with fierce staring eyes. After his first attempt to catch the bait in the centre was a failure, he flew straight at me and ripped my shirt with his talons! He was clearly cross that he was being asked to work for his food!

Eventually though, after many trial runs and many errors, Manue hit the jackpot. He snatched the fish from the little pond, the cameras fired, and we got to see the moment in perfect detail. We watched him swooping in towards the bait. As he got close,

PORTRAIT OF A PREDATOR
BALD EAGLE
(Haliaeetus leucocephalus)

Maximum size:
6.3 kilograms; wingspan 244 cm.

Range:
North America.

Deadly facts:
some large eagles are said to fly at nearly 160 kilometres an hour when dropping down to hunt. The bald eagle's nest, known as an eyrie, is reused over many years. It can be up to 6 metres deep and over a tonne in weight.

Bald eagle with prey.

his eyes locked on to it and never left it for a millisecond until his talons were engaged. At the last moment, he threw his wings back so they acted as a parachute to slow him down before snatching the food. Then he powered upwards, using all his muscular drive to force himself skywards with his heavy prize snagged in his talons. It was a genuine first, never seen before on television and utterly stunning.

YELLOWSTONE

Yellowstone was the world's first national park and though no longer the biggest, it is still utterly vast, extending into three states. In the winter this is a place that sometimes registers the coldest temperatures anywhere on the planet. It's clad in thick snow, and while tourists on skidoos zoom and roar around the popular parts of the park, some areas are totally unvisited and as wild as anywhere you'll ever see.

Call of the wild

Our main search in Yellowstone was for wolves. Wolves have been my favourite animals since I filmed them for the first time (Iberian wolves in Portugal) and was enchanted by their eyes, their howl, their social groups and their similarity to the domestic dogs I've shared my life with. Yellowstone is known as being

Above: Grey wolf.
Following pages: Steve exploring the wild expanses of Yellowstone National Park.

the best place to see wolves, as there are people here who've been tracking them for years and keep tabs on where they are.

We had a base in the snow deep in the heart of Yellowstone, camping in tents that looked like bunkers and heading out in a contraption that was basically a minibus that someone had welded a tank to the bottom of. It got through the worst of the snow without any problem. The first sign was a carcass that had clearly been killed by wolves. Wolf kills are the most distinctive of all. The pack feeds together and with a frenzy that is unrivalled. They plant their big feet down, straighten their front legs and shake their heads from side to side, creating a really gory mess. There was blood staining the snow as well as wolf tracks and droppings. We were getting closer.

PORTRAIT OF A PREDATOR

GREY WOLF (Canis lupus)

Maximum size:
80 kilograms; 1.6 metres long, with tail of 56 centimetres.

Range:
across the northern hemisphere, most numerous in Canada and Russia.

Deadly facts:
until recently nobody in the US had ever been killed by a wild wolf. Wolves were once the most widespread large carnivore on Earth, but they have been exterminated through most of their range.

The other wildlife in Yellowstone was also exceptional and even the most familiar of animals looked especially delightful in snowy surroundings. First we saw a bobcat, wandering down the edge of a frozen river, then an otter, hunting as it moved downriver, diving through holes in the ice. And at the end of the last day, we spotted a red fox hunting for lemmings beneath the snow and looking too gorgeous for words in his lush orange winter coat. He was one of the most beautiful foxes I've ever seen. A bald eagle perched in a leafless tree to survey the landscape seemed to have a magisterial arrogance.

We moved to the northern edge of Yellowstone Park where it seemed they were having more wolf sightings. On the second day of looking, we pulled into a layby where some wildlife watchers were poised with their binoculars, staring into the distance. Two wolves were striding across the snow about a mile off. They seemed to be heading west, and the park ranger who was with us had spied a spot earlier where a kill had been left, so decided to be canny and backtrack towards it. His instincts were right. We saw the wolves cross the road no more than 200 metres in front of us. It was an exciting moment for everyone, but especially for me.

Watching the bison in Yellowstone.

Deadly defender

Our next target animal was the giant of the American continent, the bison. It can be difficult to explain why an animal that is 100 per cent herbivore is Deadly, but with bison it is easy! They just look ominous and impressive.

Bison are hulking great bovids (members of the cow family), can weigh a metric tonne and have muscular humps that support their vast bony skulls. When they feel threatened, they stampede, and the very earth shakes.

A mighty bison.

These animals are the sworn foes of the wolves and do battle with them in the snows. The wolves have teamwork on their side and will select a particularly weak individual, then run it down, nipping at the animal's achilles tendons and savaging it till it eventually succumbs. The bison, for their part, have strength in numbers and will stampede, then take on a wheel formation to protect themselves, with the weakest animals protected on the inside. Bison versus wolf is one of the most dramatic of all wild conflicts.

In order to find our bison, we all put on snowshoes and started to yomp through the spruce and pine in the direction of a snowy meadow where we thought the bison would be. That turned out to be rather harder than expected. In among the trees, the snow had drifted, so in some places it was chest height. Battling through it, dragging a sled with all the camera equipment, was challenging to say the least.

By the time we found our first traces of bison, we were exhausted! The first sign was a big brown fruitcake of a cowpat – still steaming and warm enough that you could have plunged your hand into it and used it as a glove! I knew the bison could not be far away, and sure enough, just a few minutes later, we saw them, scraping the snow to get at vegetation beneath. They were close to areas of volcanic activity, where the warmth had melted enough of the white stuff to make the food accessible.

The team on the trail of bison.

SOUTHERN

STATES

Turning south, we journeyed through the United States to the forests, mountains and swamps of North Carolina and Georgia, where we encountered many kinds of reptiles and other creatures. Then on to the parched lands of Texas, the second-largest US state, and a fruitless search for mountain lions, although we were rewarded with some other star predators, including black widow spiders. In California, on the western coast, we took to the sea and enjoyed some spectacular dives with sea lions, jellyfish and super-sized sharks.

NORTH CAROLINA

Our Pole to Pole adventure was finding its way south now, into areas that during the summer are bathed in sunshine, where people come for beach holidays and to splash around in the Atlantic surf. However, we were going to be there in March, so it was still winter in the Carolinas. While doing my research, I looked up the average temperatures for the region and my heart sank. It was definitely going to be too cold and too early for much of the wildlife, most of which would still be hibernating. But the schedule couldn't change so we would have to focus on finding some animals that stay active through the winter.

A red wolf at a breeding centre.

Cry wolf

Our first target was one of the rarest canids on Earth: the red wolf. This animal was hunted to extinction in the wild in this part of the world but is making a comeback, thanks to the efforts of humans. Unfortunately we had no success at seeing the wolves running free, there are only around a hundred of them in the wild, and they are very canny and great at staying away from prying eyes! We sat out till late for several evenings, using thermal-imaging cameras and infra-red technology to try and trace them. But without any luck. To make sure that we got the animals on film, we visited a centre where biologists

are breeding red wolves for return to the wild. Even here in captivity the animals were shy and nervous, but we had the great privilege of releasing three youngsters into the wild. Seeing them running off into the woods was quite a special occasion. For me, the wilderness is not complete without its top-of-the-line predators.

North Carolina has the dubious honour of being the place in the US with the most

Above and following pages: Filming the timber rattlesnake.

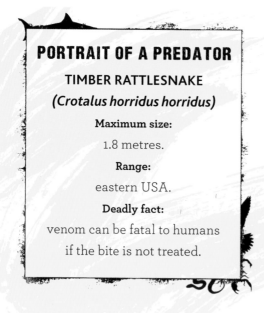

PORTRAIT OF A PREDATOR

TIMBER RATTLESNAKE
(*Crotalus horridus horridus*)

Maximum size:

1.8 metres.

Range:

eastern USA.

Deadly fact:

venom can be fatal to humans
if the bite is not treated.

venomous snakebites to human beings, so we decided to go and see if we could find any of the culprits. Unfortunately it was too early in the year and too cold, so the snakes were still hibernating. So instead I came up with the plan of filming a captive timber rattlesnake rattling in slow motion. Even that was hard at these temperatures – we had to leave the snake on a heated car seat for three hours until it even had enough energy to rattle! Once we'd managed to get the shot, it was breathtaking. Rather than shaking from side to side as you might expect, the motion ripples up and down the tail in a beautiful wave – a piece of animal behaviour that can only be seen and understood in slow motion.

Straight from hell

Our last target was up in the Smoky Mountains. We were looking for an animal that is the largest salamander in the Americas and has one of the best names of all creatures – the hellbender. Generally areas of the planet that are damp and warm provide the greatest diversity of salamander species, as these animals are cold-blooded and do a certain amount of breathing through their skin so must stay moist. However, the very largest species occur in environments just like in these mountains: chilly streams, where the water runs full of dissolved oxygen. The hellbender's body is replete with folds and flaps that extend the body's surface area and therefore the amount of skin it can absorb oxygen through.

Hellbenders can grow to be about seventy centimetres in length and their favourite prey is crayfish. They lie in wait in cracks under rocks, the flat squishy body allowing them to hide in even the most meagre of crevices. It's illegal to disturb these beasts without a licence, as they have been over-collected by the pet trade, so we joined up with a team of salamander scientists, who have been surveying hellbenders for many years.

We searched under rocks in streams fed by snowmelt all day long. Some of the rocks must have weighed a quarter of a tonne, so two or three burly guys did the lifting, while I slipped my hand underneath to see if I could grab a hellbender. I have never been so cold in my entire life. It was genuinely quite dangerous, as they were having to keep these massive boulders off me as I plunged into the icy stream underneath them. At one point the blokes lost their grip on a vast rock and it dropped down with my arm under it. I leapt back with millimetres to spare and we all looked at each other seriously. A centimetre or two either way and my arm would have been crushed.

After a couple of hours, we were all starting to think that hellbenders were genuinely a creature of myth. They certainly didn't seem to exist in this river! Then, as my face froze into a chilly mask, my fingertips clutched something underneath a rock. It was too dark and gloomy to see anything, but I had my first hellbender! I clasped my fingers around it, but there was a thrash and a twist, and it had wriggled free.

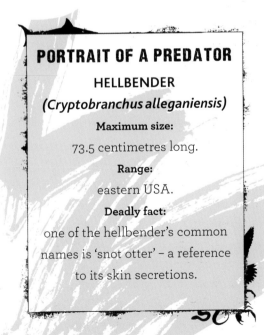

PORTRAIT OF A PREDATOR

HELLBENDER
(Cryptobranchus alleganiensis)

Maximum size:

73.5 centimetres long.

Range:

eastern USA.

Deadly fact:

one of the hellbender's common names is 'snot otter' – a reference to its skin secretions.

Steve finds a hellbender salamander.

Frantically I leapt up and started splashing around downstream hoping it had been swept that way. Nothing. The others looked at me with a mixture of amusement and annoyance. They after all were just as cold as I was!

Eventually, though, we lifted a rock and I felt something shift underneath it. As long as from my elbow to my fingertips, this weird-looking critter was a real triumph and very, very odd! It smelled very faintly of rhubarb, which is the characteristic scent of alkaloids. It was exactly the same when I filmed giant salamanders in Japan. Most likely, these mild poisons are in the animals' skin secretions and act as a deterrent to predators that might want to eat them. The hellbender has a big smiley mouth and its teeth are far from terrifying, but it can simply open its mouth to create an irresistible vacuum that sucks in food.

GEORGIA

The southern states of the US are really rich in some of my favourite animals: the reptiles. Georgia was a new state for Deadly, but had plenty of cypress swamps and forests that would be perfect places for finding reptiles. We also had the exciting opportunity to spend three days just searching the swamplands, with several animals in mind, but the strong possibility of being able to find some corking surprises too.

Cotton killer

In this part of the world, there's one snake I have a particular soft spot for. It's called the water moccasin or cottonmouth, named for the inside of its mouth, which is cotton bud white. When the snake feels threatened, it gapes, showing off the bright interior of the mouth. Many of the people who live here tend to think anything that slithers is a cottonmouth, therefore dangerous, and shoot it. On a previous trip here I hand-caught a snake on one of the rivers

PORTRAIT OF A PREDATOR

COTTONMOUTH
(Agkistrodon piscivorus)

Maximum size:
1.8 metres long.

Range:
across the southern US,
in wet and swampy habitats.

Venom:
not massively toxic to humans,
and unlikely to kill.

Deadly fact:
scientific name means 'fishhook-
toothed fish eater' which is a
clue to its diet!

here, and the fisherman with us was horrified, saying: 'What you doing? That there's a venomous cottonmouth!' It wasn't, it was a totally harmless water snake, but if it had been up to him the creature would have been killed instantly. The cottonmouth itself very rarely hurts human beings, instead hunting fish and frogs around water. In fact, there are around sixty different species of snake in this region, many of which are vaguely dark in colour and close in shape and size to the cottonmouth. This does kind of show how you need to know what you're doing when you go out catching snakes!

We were going to be searching in a cypress swamp, flooded with dark brown waters that looked like overstewed tea. The crew fanned out in a line so that we covered the maximum amount of ground. It was snake central. Every half an hour or so someone would call out 'SNAKE!' and we'd go running, converging on the spot with our cameras rolling. The snake count was really impressive, several canebrake rattlesnakes, a slew of water snakes and of course the cottonmouths. The biggest was as long as my arm, but that wasn't the one that ended up being shown in the final programme. That one was much smaller but had the brightest colours I've ever seen on a cottonmouth – orange, with brown bands and white spots. It was beautiful in its way, particularly as it swam away with a sinuous motion through the prehistoric-looking swamp.

Snapping Deadly icon
While we were off doing our snake search, we had traps in place to try to bring our next contender to us. We had first featured alligator snapping turtles way back on series one of Deadly 60, and it had proved one of the most popular of all our predators. For a start, it is the largest and heaviest freshwater turtle on Earth and its bite is the stuff of legends. The jaw has no teeth inside, but a scything cutting edge with a bite force that can splinter bone. On the tongue is a vermiform or worm-like structure. When this is engorged with blood, it becomes pink and wriggles about in the water,

Steve with a cottonmouth snake.

Big Al, the alligator snapping turtle.

enticing other predators like fish, waterbirds and frogs to swim into the turtle's mouth. They get a nasty surprise!

Sadly this time our nets didn't succeed in bringing in any snappers, but we did have a back-up plan. The local education centre had a turtle called Big Al, who'd been living there for many years. Big Al was really, well, big, at least as big as the turtle we'd caught way back on series one. I could barely lift him with both hands and had to rest the back of his shell on my thighs to hoist him out of the water. We offered him a carrot to snap and he went through it like a samurai sword! Undoubtedly deadly.

TEXAS

Known as the Lone Star state, Texas is the second largest state in the Union. You could drop the whole country of France into it and it wouldn't even touch the sides. Much of Texas is very dry, with some areas of huge desert. This is the reserve of the rattlesnake and the ranch, the steer and the scorpion, the cowboy and the copperhead. We were working on a vast nature reserve there, bordered by huge ranches. Every morning we woke up before sunrise and, bleary eyed, scanned the rocky ridges and wild gullies for our predator stars.

Gator gar

The river we were set to search has plenty of alligators and loads of venomous snakes, but instead, we were going fishing – fishing for the largest exclusively freshwater fish on the continent, the alligator gar. In order to catch a big one, we would have to get to a seriously remote section of river where other fishermen never went. Luckily, we had with us a guide who knew the wilder sections of the waterways like the back of his hand. The huge prehistoric fish we were after didn't manage to survive for over a hundred million years without being a bit canny. They won't feed if they sense boats are around, so we needed to leave bait in place, then retreat to a safe distance. Each rod had a line sensor on it, so that if a fish were to take our bait, it would start beeping, and we could come running.

It was several hours before we had any action, but when we did, it really kicked off. First one line ran, then another. We decided on the first to pull in, and I drew it in to the boat. The result was a superb alligator garfish, as long as my leg and utterly prehistoric looking. This was a total triumph. We released it into the water safe and sound, high-fiving each other with excitement, but this was only the beginning; there was another line to try.

As I drew the line in towards me, I could feel it was something different. This was a much bigger fish. I would have to be really careful about how I handled it; the line had a breaking strain of only about forty-five kilograms, and the fish would certainly weigh more than that. I had to ensure it didn't fight back

full force, or the line would snap. I reeled it in as patiently as I dared. But then suddenly, the fish lunged out of the water. We all caught our breath. It was huge. The head alone was the size of a big male crocodile. It was one of the most prehistoric sights I have ever seen. But now, we had to land it.

Fishing really isn't my thing. I have proved on many Deadly shoots in the past that I am utterly incapable when it comes to landing a fish, even small ones. It would be nuts to leave a catch like this to me, so I passed the line over to our guide, Bubba. He drew the fish in ever so carefully, while I waited with a noose of rope in order to lasso the fish as it got alongside. The gar has a mouth bristling with teeth, some of which are like its crocodilian namesake while others are long and thin and more distinctly fish-like. The beast is armoured in plate-like scales and looks like a monster out of a cartoon dinosaur picture book. It was only when it was safe alongside that we had a chance to assess how big the thing really was. Bubba measured it carefully, this could be important. It was well over two metres long, but I saw a faint look of disappointment cross his face. Turned out, we were ten centimetres short of the State record for the biggest ever alligator gar. As we watched it swim away, none the worse, it crossed my mind that this was still not bad for an angling amateur.

Copperhead

If the cottonmouth is the serpent of the swamps, the copperhead is its dry woodland equivalent.

Admiring our alligator gar!

It, too, is a viper, but much more conventional – the cottonmouth's soggy habits and fish prey are unusual. The copperhead, living in drier places and feeding on small mammals, is much more what you might expect of a viper. We found several during our trips here, but the most beautiful was in a canyon late at night. We were trekking through the still warm rock, when I saw a bright orange gleam in my torchlight. The snake was one of the most gorgeous in colour I have ever seen – three different shades of orange, from fluorescent to charred. The head was a classic viper shape, like an arrowhead, and its eyes mean-looking, with vertical pupils. The snake was making its way through a bush, probably looking for a suitable place to set up an ambush when I found it. It sat on my snake hook with remarkable calm, the very picture of grace and glory, and never threatening to strike. Beautiful.

Steve with a copperhead snake.

Cat of many names

There is one animal I always dread the researchers in the office bringing up. In South America it is known as the puma, in Florida the panther, in much of the rest of the States as a cougar or mountain lion. In fact the Guinness Book of Records marks it as the mammal with the most common names! Experience has shown me, though, that it is not an animal you can just go out and try to find in the wild. Mountain lions are around, and they are not especially rare. It's just that they do all they can to stay away from us and they are very good at it! In places where they do occur, most people live their entire lives without seeing one, or even knowing they are around.

In Texas we were hooking up with a group of biologists who had been tracking mountain lions. They had two individuals who had been fitted with radio collars, which increased our chances. Only problem was that neither of the two collared animals were within 150 kilometres of where we were based! It was going to be another slog, of getting up before dawn, setting out dozens of camera traps and working through to beyond midnight, everyone secretly suspecting that we wouldn't see anything. Eventually, after three days, we decided to give up and move on. For now, the mountain lion will have to remain my Deadly bogeyman!

Black widow

As we had little luck finding a cougar, there was a lion-sized hole in our programme, which needed filling. Luckily, I'd saved a few easier creatures as get-out-of-jail-free cards for just such an occasion. We'd never featured the black widow spider, a true Deadly icon, although we had filmed its close cousin, the redback, in Australia. The black widow earned its name from the female's habit of eating her mates. This probably doesn't happen every time they mate, but often enough to have become legend. The spider herself is a real beauty. Her abdomen is exactly pea-sized, glossy black, with markings in white and red on the underside. In some cases, the markings can resemble a human face, perhaps even a skull. She sits inside a messy white web, waiting to sense the vibration of prey.

PORTRAIT OF A PREDATOR

BLACK WIDOW SPIDER
(Latrodectus hesperus)

Maximum size:

3.8 centimetres (female).

Range:

warmer parts of United States.

Deadly fact:

venom can be 15 times more
potent than a rattlesnake's.

We'd managed to find a tumble of webs inside cactus plants close to the ranch. Each plant had at least three spiders. We'd been searching for mountain lions until late, so didn't even start filming until midnight and everyone was tired and a bit irritable, but we soon woke up. Fortunately, this is prime hunting time for the spiders. Cameraman Lucky Luke and I edged near to the webs on our bellies, not wanting to make any vibration that might scare the spider back into her little cave between the cactus stems. Three of four times we failed – the spider sensed us, and scooted straight in.

On the fourth occasion, as I inched closer, the light panel I was carrying to illuminate the whole thing attracted a flying chafer beetle. It bounced off the front of my light and into the web. Instantly, its struggles sent shockwaves through the web,

Black widow spider.

and the spider was out in a flash. Luke frantically fought to focus his macro lens (for filming small things) as she dashed towards the luckless beetle. Bam! She hit it with a couple of bites, pumping venom into her prey. Then she started teasing sheets of silk from the spinnerets at the rear of her abdomen, trussing up the beetle in a silken shroud. Every few seconds, the beetle struggled, and the spider would bite again, pumping it full of toxins that could in extreme situations kill a human or at least cause great pain. It was a magnificent example of murder in miniature.

CALIFORNIA

California is the financially richest state in the US and one of the most populated. However, despite all the humans, it's a big place and there are marvellous national parks, mountain ranges and wildlife. I decided to make the seas my focus for this programme, as the section of the Pacific that lashes these shores is bliss for animal life and much of it is Deadly.

Killer clown

California sea lions were a terrific animal to start with, partly because there is a colony right outside the city of San Diego. It's quite something to be able to dive with such a sensational predator, while tourists sunbathe no more than a stone's throw away from you! Sea lions have a reputation for being circus clowns – animals that can be trained to do complex tricks for fish rewards. In the wild, however, they are sophisticated hunters. Perhaps their finest tool is their vibrissae or whiskers. These are connected to many more nerve endings than you'd find on a cat or dog. They don't only sense the things they touch, but also the wake of fish that have already swum past, a skill that is really useful in the murky coastal waters where the sea lions fish. These are probably the fastest of all sea lions and the males particularly can get to a prodigious size. They are much larger than the females.

Despite the fact that the colony was so close to shore and to the beach, this was actually a harder task than expected. The waves were over my head and breaking on to a rocky shore. Lots of fun if you're just in your swimsuit, but

not great if you're carting around a fridge-freezer's weight of scuba tanks on your back and wearing flippers. I got absolutely smashed on to the shore, and just swimming out to where the colony was nearly burned all my air! Once we finally dropped below the surface, the sea lions themselves were nothing like as inquisitive as they usually are. I guess that comes from seeing hundreds of humans every day – they were just plain bored of people. The visibility wasn't great either. It was decent, but we knew we could do better. We would have to wait until we were across the border and a few weeks further into our trip.

Supersized stinger

My next animal was one we really hadn't expected to film. We were plodding along in our little yellow boat, when I saw a massive jellyfish from the surface and yelled out to stop. We hopped into the water wearing our scuba gear and saw a truly gorgeous black sea nettle jellyfish – pink, purple, yellow, its skirts trailing behind it for at least five metres. Looking at it closely, though,

Black sea nettle jellyfish.

I could see that something had taken some massive bites out of it, and I had an idea what. After another half an hour under steam, I spotted a flapping dorsal fin from the surface. We stopped and cameraman Luke and I jumped in. It was a sunfish. These remarkable beasties are the largest of all bony fish and feed entirely on jellyfish. I swam after this odd-looking beast with its huge bulgy eyes for what seemed like an eternity. Finally, after swimming till I was utterly exhausted, the

PORTRAIT OF A PREDATOR
BLACK SEA NETTLE JELLYFISH
(Chrysaora achlyos)

Maximum size:

bell is 91 centimetres across.

Range:

off coast of southern California and Mexico.

Deadly fact:

arms and tentacles can measure 6 metres or more.

sunfish stopped. As I came up to it, I reached out, and plucked some parasites off its skin. This is something that small cleaner fish will do, and the sunfish love it. The huge flat fish rolled over on to its side in ecstasy, loving being cleaned even though it was a human doing the cleaning!

Blue beauty and shark speedster
The main focus of my mission in these California waters, though, were some old Deadly favourites… sharks. We headed directly out to sea in our little yellow boat to a place far from land where we could put down a chum slick – a fishy mixture to attract the sharks. On the way, we came across an enormous pod of bottlenose dolphins which scorched past us at great speeds, peppering us

A mighty sunfish.

Following pages: Steve encounters a blue shark.

Filming the mako shark.

with their sonar. This was just a warm-up, preparation for what was in store later on. Our spot was about twelve kilometres offshore. We dribbled fish guts and blood into the water, creating a slick that any nearby sharks would find irresistible. It worked! Within an hour we had our first sharks: blue sharks. Lucky Luke the cameraman and I slid over the side and soon had the two blues bumping their noses off our cameras and nibbling on our fins.

Then it got even more exciting . . . two mako sharks turned up! They weren't big, perhaps as long as I am tall, but they were incredibly quick. Makos are the fastest shark on Earth and one of the fastest fish in the oceans. The half-moon shaped tail whips them up to speeds of fifty kilometres an hour, which is quicker than our boat could go! The makos were more skittish than the blues, but also much more dynamic.

Just as we thought things could get no better, a huge blue shark turned up. And he was immense, at least three metres long. This shark was

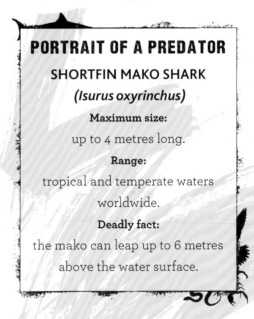

PORTRAIT OF A PREDATOR

SHORTFIN MAKO SHARK

(Isurus oxyrinchus)

Maximum size:
up to 4 metres long.

Range:
tropical and temperate waters worldwide.

Deadly fact:
the mako can leap up to 6 metres above the water surface.

friendlier than any dolphin I have ever swum with, nuzzling against me and rubbing itself on the camera, clearly relishing the electrical contact. Sharks have intensely sensitive electrical impulse sensors in their snouts, called ampullae of Lorenzini, and if you stimulate them, it hypnotises the shark. This big blue was pretty much snoring in my hands! It was one of the most enjoyable experiences I've ever had underwater. So much so that we totally lost track of time. When we got out, we finally looked at our watches. Luke and I had spent seven hours in the water with sharks!

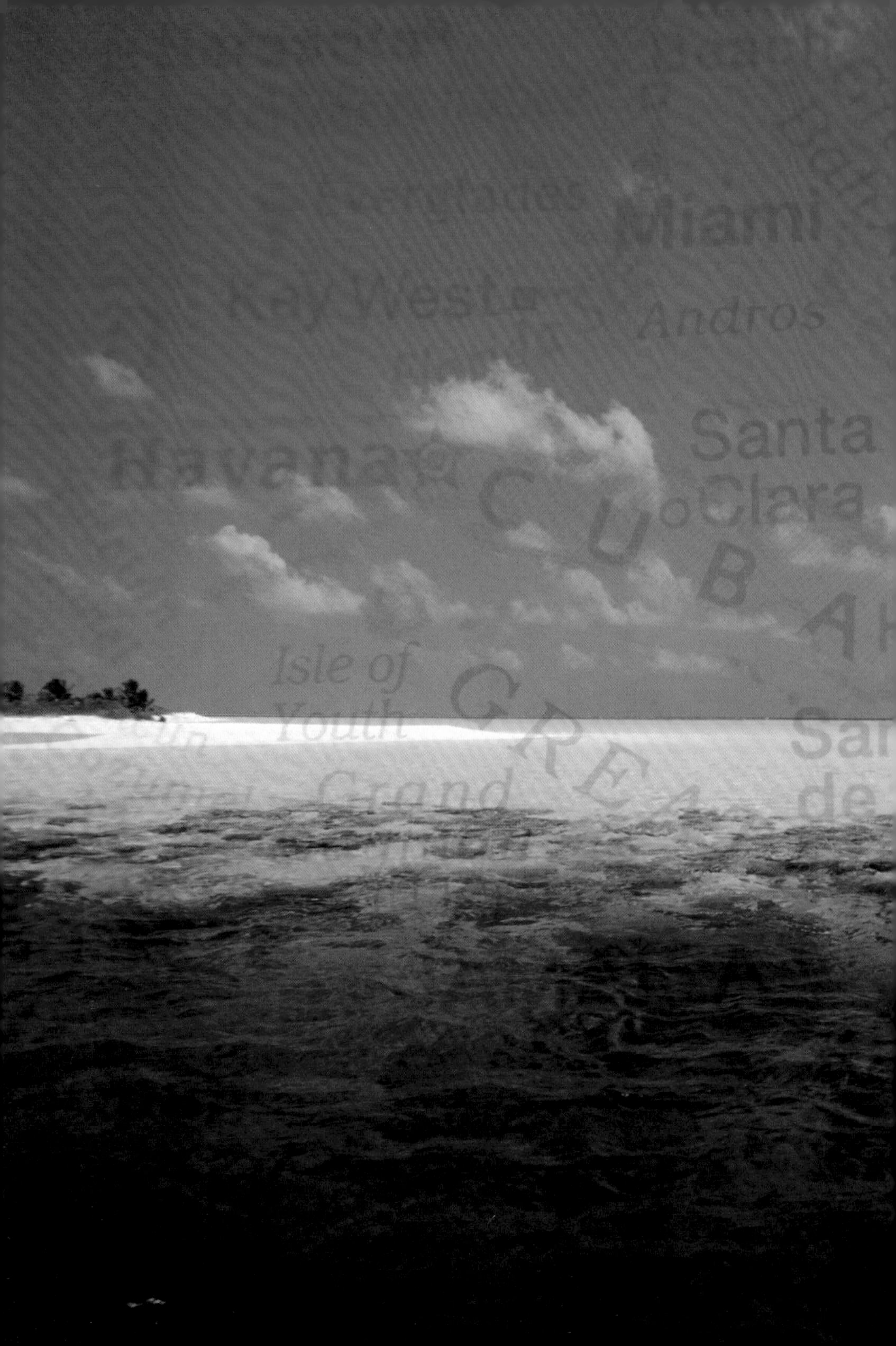
Miami
Andros
Santa
Clara
Havana
CUBA
Isle of
Youth

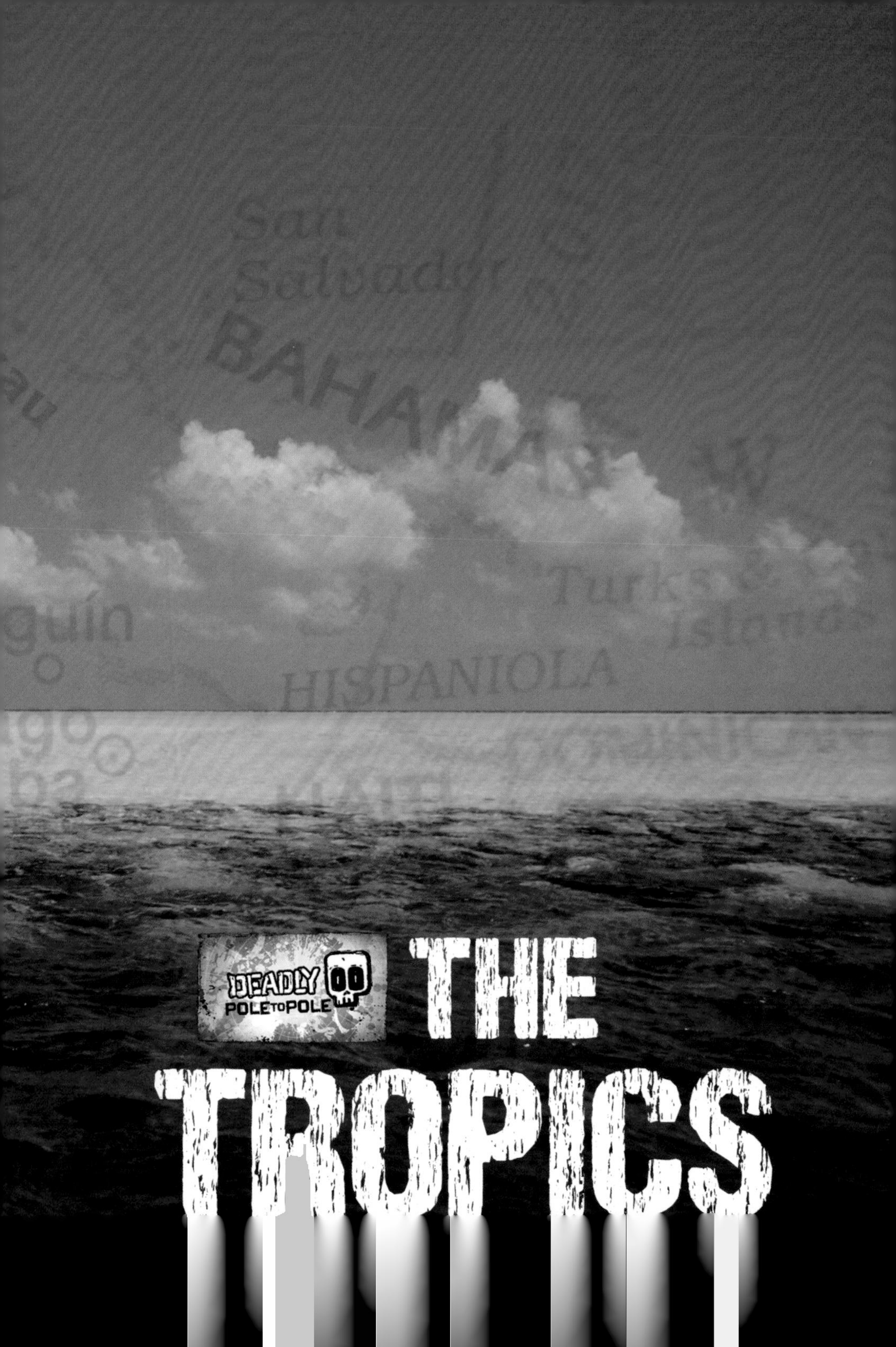

San
Salvador

BAHAMAS

Turks &
Islands

guín

HISPANIOLA

DEADLY
POLE TO POLE **THE**
TROPICS

The next part of our journey took us to the land and seas between the tropic of Cancer and the tropic of Capricorn. The area straddles the equator so has a warm climate and tends to be sunny and humid for most of the year. It includes Central America, the narrow strip of land that connects the large landmasses of North and South America, as well as the many islands in the Caribbean Sea to the east of Central America. Off the coast of North America lie the islands of Hawaii, actually the tops of volcanic mountains partially submerged in the Pacific Ocean.

BAHAMAS

The Caribbean is a favourite destination of Deadly, and not because of the sandy beaches. Way back on the very first series of Deadly, we went to a place called Tiger Beach for an extraordinary encounter with sharks. This time we were going back with the time-slice kit – a ring of cameras that we'd used for filming the bald eagle catching a fish on Vancouver Island. With this technology that was pioneered many years back for the movie *The Matrix*, we were hoping to discover the anatomy of a shark bite – and it would be the first use of the time-slice underwater.

Swimming banana

The water was alive with sharks: lemons, tigers, even a few bulls and Caribbean reef sharks. I went down with a bucket of fish. The idea was to lure the sharks in, then try to get them to bite right dead centre of the time-slice rig. We had three days to try to pull it off. Against the advice of our safety divers, I decided to wear chain mail underneath my wetsuit. It turned out to be a very good decision! The whole shoot was about trial and error. To begin with, we tried to entice a single shark, but twenty or thirty would descend on me, and I'd get swamped by them, overwhelmed in a cloud of sharks. There was too much action and chaos to get a clear shot. So we developed a method of working, where one of the safety divers would take a piece of fish and swim off like crazy, drawing

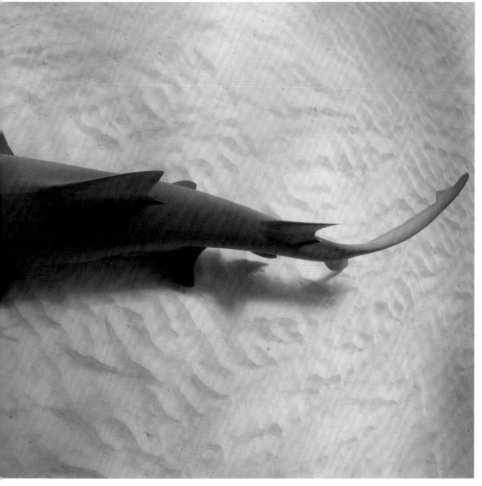

Above: Looking down on a lemon shark.
Following pages: Steve in the Bahamas, about to dive with lemon sharks.

Lemon sharks take the bait.

the majority of sharks away. Then I would try to get the shot with one of the few sharks that remained.

It was day two before we got our first decent shot: a large lemon shark chomping, its jaws distending forwards, teeth on full display, mouth opening up like a great big bucket to swallow the fish and sucking it in like a powerful vacuum cleaner. It was breathtaking. We must have nailed twenty bites over the next day.

//////// **CLOSE SHAVE** \\\\\\\\\

I'm sitting in the sweet spot, waiting for a shark, big chunk of fish in
hand. All of sudden, a shark comes from behind me, out of my view.
It chomps down not only on the fish, but also on my whole hand.
Luckily my instincts are not to pull away, but to go with it. The shark
drags me off, pulling me along bodily through the water for several
metres. I know if I try to yank away, it will shred my arm, even with
the chain mail on. Luckily, after towing me through the water for no
more than a few seconds it lets me go, as I create too much drag.
By keeping my cool, I manage to get away with just a few scratches,
and the shark has kept all of its teeth!

////////////////////////////

Sneaky tiger

The next target was the tiger shark, the animal that gives the area its name.
I spend a good deal of my time trying to tell people that sharks are not
dangerous to humans and deserve our love and care, not fear. However, that
doesn't mean they are cuddly fish that you can play around with carelessly
– and certainly not tiger sharks. They are one of the giant predatory shark
species, with double-curved serrated teeth that can cut through turtle shell.
They are also sneaky and pugnacious.

Tigers are the most omnivorous of the 450 or so species of sharks. They
will eat almost anything, from rotting whale carcasses to jellyfish, from
human debris to birds at the surface. Animals with this feeding strategy are
constantly evaluating potential food items in front of them and if you're a
diver, that can be you. You need eyes in the back of your head, as sometimes
the tiger sharks will circle behind you and try to deliver a sneaky bite. Johnny
the cameraman was holding on to the time-slice rig, when one especially

difficult tiger snuck up behind him and went for his leg. It was seconds away from taking a chunk out of his calf, before I swam in, yelling into my mask and pushed it away.

My beliefs about sharks are well known. These animals are of no statistical danger to humans worldwide. The great white shark kills an average of fewer than one person in the whole world every year. By comparison the humble honeybee kills six people in the UK alone from an allergic reaction to their sting. Falling

PORTRAIT OF A PREDATOR

TIGER SHARK
(*Galeocerdo cuvier*)

Maximum size:

7.5 metres.

Range:

tropical and subtropical seas worldwide.

Deadly fact:

teeth are curved on both sides and are often said to look like a can opener blade, ideal for carving into tough food like turtle shell.

Sneaky tiger shark.

vending machines kill more people than all the species of shark combined. However, sharks are still very big predatory fish that have the ability to bite a person in two. We need to go into every single deliberate interaction with sharks with our eyes open, and with huge amounts of knowledge, experience and respect.

Deeper underground

Believe it or not, sharks were not the scariest sequence we had planned in the Bahamas. We were going on a mission into the dark underworld that lies beneath the islands. The caves here, though, are not filled with air but flooded with water. Cave diving is one of the most dangerous activities on Earth. If you run out of air or light or get lost you will die. It's that simple. For this reason I was suggesting caves as a Deadly environment, a Deadly place, and they certainly lived up to their reputation. I have been diving for 22 years and logged thousands of hours underwater, but I needed special training in a bunch of flooded mines in Wales (in the middle of winter!) in order to be able to do these dives. There was snow on the ground and carrying my tanks and equipment up a mountain in order to dive into freezing water was particularly unpleasant. It was all a million miles away from the warm clear waters of the Bahamas, but the techniques I learned would be the only thing that would keep me alive.

I've also been really claustrophobic with caves ever since an expedition into an unexplored cave system in Borneo where I got stuck, days and days away from help. My caving buddy Tim told me he'd have to leave me there for a few days until I lost some weight. And he meant it. Somehow after that I managed to breathe out enough to squeeze myself free! To try to get through these cave systems where there is no air whatsoever would be a real mindgame for me.

The dives began in an innocuous little pool, no bigger than a couple of bathtubs. It gave no indication of the vast expanses of cavern that lay beyond. The caves were filled with water with almost infinite visibility,

so clear that it felt like flying rather than diving. The stalactites and stalagmites were like the columns on some mighty sunken Coliseum, and they had a grandeur and wonder I have never experienced before.

Soon all natural light was left behind, and we started to find evidence of troglodytes: cave-living beasts. There were tiny shrimps which scampered over to pick pieces of loose skin from my hands, and a remipede, kind of like a swimming centipede, but dating back hundreds of millions of years. These bizarre almost transparent creatures flail about in the water and have fangs that may secrete venom for tucking into the few other organisms that live here. Even more sinister was a fish called a cave brotulid that is again probably impossibly ancient. It has milky eyes and a massive bulbous mouth, which can swell to many times its original size in order to take in huge food items. Deep inside there was evidence of more ancient life – a crocodile skull. The croc would have crawled inside to die at least 8,000 years ago, when sea levels were much lower and these caves were totally dry. It seemed to be grinning at me from the murk, like some weird Halloween horror show, making the place feel like a drowned museum vault.

As we penetrated several hundred metres inside, we got into the real danger zone. Here we had to be really careful about monitoring our air consumption; there always has to be more than enough for the return journey, and you have to be able to save yourself if anything goes wrong. We found a gargantuan room, where the stalagmites that came up from the floor were smoothed by the imperceptible movement of water over millennia and had become like statues of people. It was just how I imagined the scene in Narnia, where the white witch has frozen humans and animals in stone and they stand there transfixed for all eternity. It was one of the most dramatic and spellbinding things I've ever been privileged to witness, but I have never been so overjoyed to see the sunlight on my return!

Cave diving – Steve in the first of the pools.

CUBA

This was the first time I'd visited Cuba, isle of salsa, classic cars and Castro. It's a stunning place, historically isolated from the United States despite being only a matter of kilometres away from it. Because of its isolation, Cuba has retained its own character. We'd come here for marine marvels and also for a subterranean spectacle, which occurred just a few hours from the capital of Havana.

Hanging serpent

Two hours' drive and a half hour's stroll from the island's capital, we reached

Cuban boa.

an innocuous slice in a bunch of rocks among some farmer's fields. The caves were not much to look at, but what lay inside was a true marvel. Hundreds of thousands of bats roosted within, but it was not them we had come here to see. We were looking for the Cuban boa, which is endemic to the island.

It took us an hour of slogging deep into the cave before we found the roosting bats. We'd been told that the snakes would be found only at the place with the highest concentration of bats. Here, the temperature soared, warmed by the body heat of the flying mammals. We all broke out in sweat and shuddered at the cockroaches and tarantulas swarming over our feet. Then suddenly, there were the snakes, clustered together in a big reptile ball. The boas hang down into the cave and, as a bat strikes them, they lash out and catch it in their needle-like teeth. Boas are constrictors, and studies have shown that such snakes can sense the heartbeat of prey, wrapped in their coils. Once the heart stops beating, the snake stops squeezing, thus saving energy.

Big mouth strikes again

Out on the marine reserve Jardines de la Reina we found ourselves in total paradise. Our home was a three-storey boat, moored above a beautiful coral reef. All we had to do was throw a few scraps overboard and silky sharks would come rushing up to get stuck into them. However, the big fish we were hoping to film would boss the sharks around, sending them packing with its massive sonic boom. It was the goliath grouper, the biggest mouth on the reef. When we dived to a glorious coral outcrop, the groupers were soon evident. There were several different species, but it was the goliaths that ruled. A truly massive fish, a goliath can get to 455 kilograms in weight, with a mouth that looks as if it could swallow a basketball whole.

In order to really appreciate the bite of the grouper, we had a camera with slow-motion capabilities. I would take down a whole lobster and try to feed

Following pages: Goliath grouper.

the grouper, at which time we'd fire off the slow-mo camera and see the whole process step by step – the lobster, by the way, was already dead. It was trickier than it sounded. There were several grouper around and they'd bully each other and the sharks out of the way, then lurk just on my shoulder out of my peripheral vision. Just when I'd made up my mind that they weren't going to play ball, one would emerge and suck the lobster down in one vast gulp. It was extraordinary watching it back in slow motion. The fish's whole jaw distended outwards, before the vacuum caused in the gaping hole left behind sucked the food in.

If the fish felt at all boxed in by the sharks or other groupers, they would unleash an incredible booming sound, twanging the muscles around their swim bladder. The boom would travel through the water as a sound wave that I could clearly feel in my stomach! After a while, the groupers got bolder,

Steve swimming with an American crocodile.

and would come in for the food as soon as I took it out of the box. Finally, the biggest grouper, who'd been keeping his distance, came and hovered in front of me, using small movements of his pectoral fins to hold station. However, this big fella was not going to wait until I wanted to feed him. The second I opened the feed box he was on me and gulped in, sucking my hand into his mouth! If I hadn't been strong and braced backwards, he would have swallowed my whole hand! My wrist was a bit scuffed up from his small teeth, but no real harm done.

Croc shock

When I proposed Cuba as a destination, my heart was set on filming the Cuban crocodile, a species that only occurs here and is known for being the most athletic of all crocs. But when genius director Rowan was researching the stories, he found we could go one better. In Cuba, there is a spot where you can dive with the largest species on the continent, the American crocodile. There are several kinds of croc that can live in either fresh or saltwater, secreting excess salt through special glands in the mouth. Here, the crocs can be found out among the coral islands and seagrass of the same marine reserve where we were filming goliath grouper.

CLOSE SHAVE

Our boatman Noah has been diving in one spot for several years and knows the crocs by name! As we arrive, he starts calling out 'Niño' in a loud deep bellow. This means 'boy', and is his name for an especially sizeable reptile. It seemed bizarre that he could call out, and a croc would come swimming, but that's exactly what is happening. Not one, but two crocs swim out of the nearby mangroves and over to the side of our small skiff. They react very quickly to movements of my hand in the water, which is a little nerve-wracking. We're hoping they won't do the same when we get in alongside them.

To distract their attention from us, we throw a piece of chicken away from the boat, and drop over the side, cameras clasped at the ready. The crocs instantly turn back towards us and make a beeline straight for me. Somewhat more disconcerting, the largest animal ducks down to the bottom and a cloud of sediment billows into the water, making the croc invisible. Eventually I manage to discern its outline beneath me. It is practically resting its head in my lap. I don't dare move – crocs will lash out at unexpected contact to their snout. Instead, I just sit there motionless, barely wanting to breathe. 'Throw a bit more chicken away from the boat', I whisper through gritted teeth to Rowan. He manages to distract the croc, and I escape with all my bits intact, but it feels like a very close shave!

HAWAII

Stranded in the midst of endless miles of Pacific blue, Hawaii is the most remote island chain on Earth. The islands themselves are volcanic and have popped up from the sea bed along the line of a hot spot, a place where molten magma comes close to the Earth's surface and occasionally surges up, creating volcanoes and eventually new islands.

We'd decided to feature this land-creating Deadly force of nature and headed out on a boat to a spot where the lava poured from vents by the sea, disgorging its orange cargo into the waves. The sea spouted violent plumes of steam where the hot rock met water. It was a fierce, elemental place, which must look something like the Earth did at its very inception. Our next step was to approach the lava up close and try to measure quite how hot it was. We managed to get a temp of 1,100 degrees centigrade! However, this whole sequence was most memorable for researcher Toby running across the black landscape to grab a camera and coming within millimetres of leaping into a still liquid floe, with a thin crust over the top hiding its lethal secret. He's one of the cleverest men I know, but it was a decidedly narrow escape!

Measuring the temperature of the lava.

Next we took a helicopter up to the caldera of the volcano itself. Our pilot was pretty confident, so we hovered alongside the circular crater, watching the yellow lava slopping around like burning treacle. You could feel the heat, despite the whirring rotors of the helicopter. The thought of what would happen if the helicopter went down sent a chill right through me. Then the pilot shouted into the intercom, 'We have a fault on one of the engines. I'm going to have to shut her down.' This had to be a joke. It was just the kind of thing a macho pilot would do to spook his tourist customers. But no, he was serious! I did my best not to panic, as he peeled away from the volcano and made for the airbase, his jaw gritted with determination, as he concentrated on the job in hand. I have never been so happy to land in my entire life!

Following pages: Approaching the bubbling lava.

Endangered hunter

Most of our mission in Hawaii was based out at sea. The Pacific Ocean that smashes against the shore is the biggest on Earth, and here is at its most abundant. However, we were in search of a rare shark, the oceanic whitetip, which in some parts of its range has lost 98 per cent of its numbers to humans, and here in Hawaii may have lost 70 per cent. These sharks are true wanderers of the open ocean and, as they may go for days without food, are hard-wired to investigate everything in their world to find out if it might be edible. Only thing is that sharks don't have fingers, so they investigate things the only way they know how – with their teeth.

Oceanic whitetips are closely related to great white sharks; in fact, an alternative common name is the lesser white shark. They have teeth that are adapted to slicing through substantial prey as well as scavenging for garbage, and they are very much a force to be reckoned with. Their reputation for being the first to arrive at a sinking ship may be slightly overstated, but of all the sharks on Earth, this is probably the one you have to respect most.

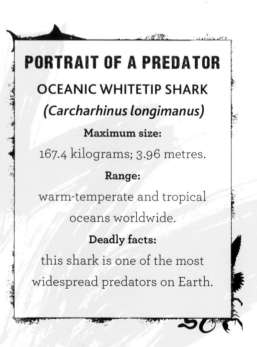

PORTRAIT OF A PREDATOR

OCEANIC WHITETIP SHARK
(*Carcharhinus longimanus*)

Maximum size:
167.4 kilograms; 3.96 metres.
Range:
warm-temperate and tropical oceans worldwide.
Deadly facts:
this shark is one of the most widespread predators on Earth.

To find an oceanic whitetip is a difficult task. They cruise the big blue, which is simply vast. To concentrate your search, what you need to do is find a regular food source for them, which, bizarrely, is pilot whales. The sharks don't hunt

Filming an oceanic whitetip shark.

these large, dark, toothed whales but probably feed on the scraps they leave behind. They even feed on their poo!

So there we were, out at sea in search of pilot whales. But the weather was not on our side and huge waves were crashing over the front of our boat, threatening to wash us all overboard. Day one was brutal and we battled to film anything at all as we were smashed around like soaking wet rag dolls. We did encounter a couple of groups of pilot whales, but they powered past us, clearly not interested in interacting, and there was nothing following them. Day two was even less promising, with higher seas and strong winds. We saw nothing at all, and director Rachel and Toby both had an extreme battle trying to keep all the cameras working in the constant spray. Perhaps this had been a gamble too far?

On the third and final day, our luck changed. We awoke to clear skies and no wind. The sea was flat. As we set out from the harbour, we all vowed one

The shark boat in Hawaii.

thing: we would be out until the sun sank below the horizon and we could go on no longer. We would find a shark!

We scoured the seas for most of the morning but saw nothing. We did, however, pull up at several buoys anchored a kilometre or so out. It's remarkable how effective these simple devices are at attracting life. Simply the shelter of a buoy at the surface and a line below it brings in thousands of fish. Beyond it the sea is empty, while beneath the water is as packed as a tropical coral reef!

Mid afternoon, just as we were starting to think we would have to turn for home, we glimpsed some dark dorsal fins surging towards us. Pilot whales! Cameraman Luke and I slipped on our masks and fins, then rolled overboard. The pilot whales were going at a great whack and again passed us on into the deep. Nothing. Our efforts had been for nothing. And then one of the guys on deck shouted out. 'Shark! Other side of the boat! I'm sure it's a shark!'

Luke and I ducked under the boat and swam in the direction he had been pointing in. Sure enough, from the crystal-clear blue waters, a shape appeared. It was an oceanic whitetip. And as it approached, another appeared, this one with several stripy pilot fish riding the bow wave at its nose. Two oceanic whitetips! This was phenomenal, but now we would have to have our wits about us. The sharks circled, getting ever closer, occasionally nosing in to bump us with their snouts. They were clearly testing out the cameras, sensing the electrical pulses coming off them and trying them out to see if they might be good to eat.

The sharks were utterly beautiful, but also pugnacious and tenacious. On several occasions we had to bump them off with the cameras, or they would have taken a little tester bite of us. Finally, after nearly an hour of them swimming around us, I decided that they had taken too much time out from searching for food. In order that they didn't leave hungry,

Eupithecia, the carnivorous caterpillar.

I fed our remaining shark a large dead fish. It scoffed it down right in front of my camera lens, showing off the teeth that so resembled those of their great white cousin. One of the undoubted triumphs of the series.

Macabre maggot

The next animal was another first for Deadly, and one I hadn't even heard of! It is called *Eupithecia* and it's a caterpillar with a difference. While the 120 thousand or so species of moth and butterfly around the world all feed on plants in their larval stage, this curious loner is a carnivore caterpillar! The tiny, camouflaged larvae lie alongside leaves, their green colours helping them to blend with their background. At the rear end is a single hair. If a small flying insect should wander past this hair and brush against it, it triggers the caterpillar to fire backwards, catching the bug in a spiky basket of legs. The caterpillar then devours its catch alive, which is all pretty grisly!

In order to see this spectacle in miniature play out, we brought along a special camera, which can not only magnify the action, but also play it back in super slow mo. I tried tickling the caterpillar with an eyelash glued to a matchstick. It instantly fired back with its lethal stabbing basket, grasping for the prey it thought was passing by!

Devil fish

Our next wild wonder was a large relative of the sharks that feeds on the smallest of aquatic organisms and is certainly no danger to us humans – the magnificent manta ray. This giant fish is incredibly graceful and has an ethereal beauty beyond compare. I'm sure I've said this enough by now, but

Steve and a manta ray.

Deadly is not about animals that are dangerous to humans, it's about animals that are deadly in their own world. And manta rays are deadly to little tiny baby sea creatures! Zooplankton is mostly made up of the larval forms of many other sea animals, such as corals, sponges and fish. The sunfish, for example, which can grow into the largest bony fish on Earth, starts life as a tiny egg, and then a planktonic larva.

PORTRAIT OF A PREDATOR

MANTA RAYS (*Manta birostris* and *Manta alfredi*)

Maximum size:
2 tonnes in weight;
up to 7 metres across

Range:
temperate, sub-tropical and tropical waters in all oceans.

Deadly fact:
largest of all ray species.

Manta rays filter plankton out of the water, using special spongy structures on their gills called rakers. They sweep through the water with their mouths open, channelling tonnes of water through their body and out of the gills. Any food gets caught on the rakers.

Usually you encounter mantas by searching for a cleaning station, a place where they come to be picked clear of parasites by little fussing cleaner wrasse. Here in Hawaii, though, they make life easy for manta spotters. By taking down a crate of dive lights to the bottom of the sea, they create an artificial bloom of plankton, which the mantas come to feed on. If you saw one of these big beasts on a dive, you'd think it had been a lucky day. As I swam through the inky dark waters towards the light, I became aware of shadowy cloaks swooping through the beams. Mantas! Lots of them! In fact, I counted over thirty! They barrel-rolled through the clouds of plankton, feasting on thousands of baby animals with every single mouthful, clattering us out of the way if we weren't careful!

Moray play

We just needed one more animal to make our stay in Hawaii complete and that was to be the marvellous moray eel. There are about 200 species found around the world, and many of them are right here in Hawaii's rich waters. On a single coral head we counted five different species. Some had crunchy molar-like teeth for munching hard-bodied prey, while others had spiky teeth that acted as a trap for snagging slippery fish that swim past their holes. Our idea was to see if we could bite test a moray eel – something that had never, to our knowledge, been tried.

Easier said than done, though. We knew our normal broad strip of rubber would be too wide for a moray to fit in its mouth, so we needed something smaller. Our solution appeared to be a bite gauge that looked more like a lipstick and would certainly fit. Our first few morays could not have been less interested and just withdrew into their holes. But one big grumpy moray

Above: Testing the strength of a moray's bite.
Following pages: Tail fluke of a magnificent humpback whale.

liked the look of the bite gauge so much, it grabbed it and yanked it back into its hole… hard! It was almost impossible to prevent myself being dragged in after it! The bite had been so powerful, we thought it must surely have registered a record-breaking bite, but I looked at the gauge nonplussed. Nothing! Then I realised why. The moray's teeth were so sharp they had severed right through the rubber. It was broken. Yet another bite test gauge destroyed by an animal!

Heat run

There is only one animal that could, and would, be with us for the entirety of our Pole to Pole journey: the mighty, planet-spanning humpback whale. We saw humpbacks feeding way up in the high Arctic, then kayaked among them in Alaska, and it is entirely possible we would meet them again way down in Antarctica. Here in Hawaii, the Alaskan whales come for their summer fun. They feed up north, then come south to breed. Only thing is that each female is so attractive to the boys that she acquires a bevy of suitors, who pursue her for many miles in a fierce furore known as the heat run. Males have even killed each other in the chase.

It was our goal to film the heat run underwater, while free diving, as there was simply no way we'd be able to kit up in our scuba gear in time. What's more, we would not be manoueverable enough to drop in and keep out of the way of the whales, who would be too caught up in their chase to watch out for us. One careless swipe of a tail from an animal that could weigh forty tonnes could easily kill a human, so we would need to keep our wits about us.

The amount of activity was extraordinary. People travel halfway round the world to see a single whale. We lost count of the humpbacks within an hour or so. They were on the horizon, spouting, breaching, smashing the water with their tails, before finally giving chase to a female. We dropped in over and again. The visibility was superb and the whales were everywhere, but they powered along at such a speed that they were simply impossible to predict.

When we stopped for lunch, something extraordinary happened. We could hear whale song. Humpbacks are the most vocal of all whales, with gorgeous sumptuous songs, which can carry for many miles. However, it's very special to hear that sound above the surface. The railings of the boat were vibrating to the sound so we realised there must be a whale underneath us! Underwater cameraman Simon and I dropped overboard to see what we could see. The whale was right under us, but at about thirty metres. I free-dived down and saw that he was hanging vertically in the water, so I just couldn't get the whole animal in shot.

Later on in the day we had more luck. We had been tailing a heat run group, with the males battering each other in their efforts to get to the big female, who was swimming away from them. We predicted where we thought the run would go and slipped in ahead of them. About ten whales came out of the blue and past us. As they went, one male smashed another with his tail, beating his rival with enormous force. They trailed streams of silvery bubbles from their blowholes as they went, disappearing into the distance. Amazing.

GUADALUPE ISLAND
Twenty-four hours hard sailing off the Pacific coast of Mexico is Guadalupe Island, a volcanic monolith that rises up out of the ocean like some kind of slumbering monster. However, it's what's beneath the waves that is truly monstrous. Guadalupe is the best place on the planet to see the true icon of Deadly, the great white shark. Not only that, but it is currently the only location where you can encounter a great white outside of a cage. It is quite simply the finest shark encounter on Earth.

Guadalupe fur seals
These seals are assumed to be the reason great whites occur here in such numbers. They are one of the smaller seal species, quite dark in colour, and with huge dark eyes. However, their behaviour is unlike that of most

Following pages: Steve diving with Guadalupe fur seals.

of the other seal species I've been lucky enough to dive with. They hang at the surface with their heads hanging down into the water, eyes looking downwards for the looming shape of a shark. They rarely stray far from the safety of the shallower waters during the day, instead heading out to hunt at night, when the sharks seem to be less interested in mammal prey.

This was to be our first dive outside of the cage in Guadalupe, but we were close enough to the coast that we didn't feel threatened. The water clarity was quite exquisite, and with bright orange garibaldi fish swimming among the swaying kelp it felt like a dive in the world's finest aquarium. It took the seals a while to get up some guts and swim in to investigate us, but when they did, they were a true wonder of the natural world. They twisted and spiralled with infinite grace and control, coming to look at themselves in the reflective glass of my mask. It was one of the most beautiful and life-affirming dives I have ever done, yet always with the knowledge of what these seals had to face every day of their lives just to stay alive.

PORTRAIT OF A PREDATOR

GREAT WHITE SHARK
(Carcharodon carcharias)

Maximum size:

up to 6.4 metres.

Range:

all oceans.

Deadly facts:

can swim at speeds of up to 50 kilometres an hour.

Great white shark

The great white is probably the most feared animal on Earth, one which has never recovered from the bad image it was given in Peter Benchley's film *Jaws*. These sharks do not live up to their reputation, being of very little threat to humans around the world. That said, this beast is a masterpiece of evolution, a creature that has purified in purpose over many hundreds of millions of years and is now a sublime predatory machine. The mouth contains 300 teeth, which are genuinely as sharp as a knife blade and hard as steel. If teeth break off they are replaced with more lined up behind them, allowing each shark to go through 30,000 teeth in a lifetime.

After a long crossing, we finally arrived at Guadalupe early in the morning, and dropped anchor in a flat calm bay. Signs were instantly good, as a pod of bottlenose whales cruised past – the first I have ever seen. The fur seals were keeping close to the coves and only visible through binoculars. As soon as we were in position, we started throwing fish chum overboard – a mixture of fish blood and oils – to coax the sharks to come and investigate. We got our first big fish mid-morning, and dropped the shark cage over the side.

Safely in the shark cage.

Though our plan was to try to dive with great whites out in blue water, we
needed the cage to assess the behaviour and personality of each individual
shark. It may seem crazy that you can suss out the character of a fish, but
they give you very definite signals. A shark that is calm and relaxed has
its pectoral fins spread wide like wings, its profile sleek and straight, tail
movements lazy and languid. This would be the kind of shark we needed.
On the other hand, if the shark has its gills billowing, back arched, pectoral

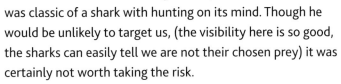

fins dropped and mouth open, it is ready for action. If a shark like this was around, we would be staying firmly inside the cage.

Unfortunately, our first shark fell firmly into the second category. He was a small male, maybe three metres long, but his whole attitude felt like trouble. He was sneaking around behind the cages, before lunging towards the bait we had placed in the water ahead of us. The angular, unpredictable movement

was classic of a shark with hunting on its mind. Though he would be unlikely to target us, (the visibility here is so good, the sharks can easily tell we are not their chosen prey) it was certainly not worth taking the risk.

The light faded on our first day far too quickly. The following day would be our only full day working with the sharks, leaving us under tremendous pressure. This was one of the only times that we had gambled on having a whole programme based around one animal, and with so little time, every second was critical. The last thing we needed was to be thinking more about making the programme and getting the shots than about whether a shark was the right one.

Next morning, I was down on my knees on the back deck, hurling fish goo overboard from very first light, desperate to bring in the sharks. Unfortunately, it seemed they had better things to do. We had a couple of vaguely interested swim-bys, but they just carried on gliding off into the big blue. It got towards late afternoon, and we still hadn't filmed anything at all, and we would have to leave Guadalupe the following morning. There was no more than an hour of sunlight left, when a shark turned up. Unfortunately, whoever was manning the bait had dozed off, and the shark came in and swallowed

Out in open water with a great white shark.

the whole tuna fish in one mouthful! It was a huge shark which was a good thing, but we just had to hope it hadn't filled itself up. Luckily, it came back.

We dropped into the cage as slowly and carefully as we possibly could so our bubbles wouldn't scare the shark away. My heart was thumping so hard I could hear it! I forced myself to breathe more slowly, bringing my heartrate down, trying desperately to relax. I focused on the huge fish, doing circuits round and round our cage. It was moving slowly, predictably, and had all the hallmarks of the right kind of great white for us to swim with. As I looked to the crew, I got the nod from my safety diver, from Johnny the cameraman, and over the intercom from the others up on the deck of our boat. This was the moment. I slid back the door of the cage. There was now nothing between us and the deep blue sea – and the enormous great white shark circling beyond. First I checked my buoyancy and air, forcing myself to run through all my safety checks and make sure I was OK. It was time.

I swam out as the shark came round towards the bait. It barely seemed to notice me, instead nosing up towards the chunk of dead fish at the surface. Time and again the mighty ancient predator looped around us, not showing even a single sign of aggression. She was mesmerising, bedecked in the classic countershading coloration, found in most shark species and so many other ocean predators, in which the upper surface is grey-blue and the underside is white. That way if you look down on the animal from above it blends in with the deep ocean beneath, but if you look up at it from underneath, the pale white is camouflaged against the bright sky.

After maybe half an hour, our air ran low and we had to return to the surface, but we knew we had our programme and had just undertaken something genuinely special. My love and respect for this stunning beast had grown still more, my fear for them even more rationalised.

An awe-inspiring encounter with a great white shark.

SOUTH
AMERICA

South America is the fourth largest continent and one of the most incredible places on Earth for wildlife. It extends more than 7,500 kilometres from the tropics to its tip in the chilly South Atlantic, not far from the Antarctic Circle. Its natural wonders include the Andes, the world's longest mountain range, and the Amazon, the largest of all rainforests and these varied landscapes are home to a huge range of animal species, such as jaguars, piranhas, harpy eagles and caiman.

GUYANA

Guyana is to me the most exciting of all jungle nations. It is almost the size of Britain, but has a population smaller than Birmingham's, mostly living on the coast near the capital town of Georgetown. The rest of the country is covered in rainforest that is more perfect than just about anywhere I've seen. On one of my finest ever expeditions, our team described new species here, and there is no doubt that there are thousands more still to be found.

It's been half a decade since I was last here, and I was kind of dreading coming back. Rainforests are disappearing at a terrifying rate, and my worry was that Guyana might have been spoiled since my last travels. However, as the small plane took off and headed south, the familiar excitement began to build in my stomach. We were no more than ten minutes out of Georgetown and below us was thick, thick forest. There were a few more mining camps by the banks of the huge chocolate-coloured rivers than before, and there were some gaps in the forest for logging, with tiny roads trickling through the trees to take out the biggest trees. However, once we were over the densest forest, we flew for an hour, perhaps 150 kilometres, without seeing any sign of a human being.

Finally, reptilian mountain tops began to grow from the lowlands. Steep-sided and covered with jungle, they would, I knew from experience, contain some of the most inhospitable and impenetrable terrain on Earth. My excitement built even further. We landed at a dusty airstrip, pulling in a fiercely tight turn that threw all of us back into our seats. Local kids waited at the side of the airstrip, watching bemused as we unloaded our camping and filming gear before the plane flew out low over our heads.

Epic eagle

The first mission was to film a real jungle icon: the harpy, largest eagle in the Americas and heaviest in the world. It was a serious challenge, but we were ahead of the game. A local contact had found a nest and knew that a young but well-developed chick was staying around the area while he was being raised by his parents. Harpies are reliant on their parent birds for a very long time and may still be in the nest tree a year after they've hatched! The reason for this is simple. Harpy eagles catch mammals up in the treetops, and this is one of the hardest skills for a bird of prey to learn. Imagine swooping into crowded spiky branches, flying at maybe 65 kilometres an

hour, before stabbing your talons into a fast-moving prey. It takes a long time for the youngsters to learn their trade. Monkeys and sloths are the prime targets, though sometimes the eagles may sweep down to the forest floor and catch deer.

Our young bird was around four months old, which meant he would already have fledged – gained his flight feathers – and was capable of flight. We desperately hoped not to spook

Harpy eagle.

him from the tree, but as we crept in on the forest floor, doing our best to be utterly silent, we heard vast wingbeats overhead. The chick had heard us and flown. This was worrying. If the chick could fly well, there was much less chance of him sticking around. And what we really wanted was to catch the adult birds coming in to feed him, dragging a huge mammal carcass with them. At this stage of the chick's development, that might only happen once every four or five days, and we only had three.

Anyway, we could only work with the cards we'd been dealt, so we set to frantically rigging the ropes I would use to get up into the tree. First, we used a massive catapult and fired a thin line over a high branch. Then we tugged up a thicker line that we would be able to ascend. Finally, we hung two people's bodyweight on the rope to make sure the branch was thick and strong enough to hold us, before I started my first ascent. The ropes brought me to just above the nest, and perhaps ten metres away. I hauled up some boards and made myself a makeshift seat, then hid behind a barrier of branches and leaves and prepared for a long, long wait.

My perch was perhaps forty metres up, and I hung there in my harness for thirteen hours. There was absolutely no sign of the chick. Glumly I descended, and we walked the hour and a half back to the road, then drove for another hour and a half back to the camp. It was a long slog, in hammering rain, but brightened by the appearance of one of the region's most impressive snakes: a yellow-tailed cribo. It slid off at great pace, and I had to charge through the undergrowth to grab it as it lunged out, trying to get a bite on me. The cribo isn't venomous, and a bite wouldn't be dangerous, but it has some of the strongest jaws of any snake and probably the most powerful bite. There was no doubt it would hurt if I did get nailed! Cribos are gorgeously coloured, with a slaty grey back and golden amber tail. They are also a great Deadly

PORTRAIT OF A PREDATOR

HARPY EAGLE (Harpia harpyja)

Maximum size:

wingspan 2.24 metres;
weight 9 kilograms (female).

Range:

undisturbed forest in
Central and South America.

Deadly facts:

like all mammal-eating eagles,
the harpy has short, stout talons to
punch through fur and skin. Fish
feeders have much thinner pointy
talons to grasp slippery fish.

contender, as they feed on other snakes, even some of the most venomous in the whole world!

The following morning we had to repeat the drive and walk, but started at 3.30am, as we needed to be in place before first light. This travelling back and forth was clearly a waste of time, so we decided that from then on, the team would camp by the tree and I would sleep up the tree itself. First, though, I would have to get through another day hanging in my harness. By now, the straps had started to chafe all the skin off

Top: Steve finds a yellow-tailed cribo. Bottom: Guyana base camp.
Following pages: Steve on his treetop perch.

my waist, and I was utterly bored. Another thirteen-hour day, and we had to face the fact that the bird might not be coming back. We could hear it calling somewhere nearby, but it wasn't going to come back in the dark, so we put together our sleeping arrangements. We hauled a sort of hanging tent into the canopy and started prepping it for a night out. However, as I began, the heavens opened in the way they do only in the rainforest. Within seconds I was drenched to the skin and I had no other clothes to sleep in. Even worse, I felt a gurgle in my stomach as I was fixing my dangling bed. Oh dear, this was not going to be good.

Finally, in the pitch black, I swung into the teetering bed. I was soaked, the mossies were eating me alive, I would have to sleep in my harness, and I needed the toilet. Desperately. There was nothing for it. I hung myself out the back of my hammock, hitched my harness up and my trousers down, then squirted into open air, just like the harpy eagles do themselves, to propel their droppings clear of their nests. It was up there with the most miserable nights of my life. Every fifteen minutes or so I'd have to leave the dry and dangle out over open air to relieve myself. I could have just had a little cry.

The morning bought little relief. I could hear the team on the ground, eating nice food, sitting comfortably with their hands behind their heads. I just had to dangle there. Then there was a crackle on the radio. 'Steve, Steve! It's there! Just above you!' Ever so slowly, I hitched myself upwards so I could get a different view. With a few metres gained, it was suddenly clear. The chick was sitting directly above the nest, looking around him with his eagle eyes, ever vigilant for the presence of danger or prey. Moving a millimetre at a time so as not to scare him, I lifted my video camera and propped it on a branch to get a good brace. Then I pressed record. He sat there still for a good few minutes, before finally lifting his tail and squirting a big poo – with much more grace than I had been doing all night! This is a sure sign with birds that they are about to fly, as they are lightening the load before take off. And sure enough, just seconds later he took to the air, all caught on camera. I had worked for this shot like never before, and been through real horrors, but it was worth it.

Zany zapper

Our mission now was to head far upstream, into even more remote jungle. It was a six-hour boat ride, which eventually brought us into a quiet and clear creek. Our boatmen had been here before many times and found us an idyllic spot to camp. It was right by the riverside, underneath a divine falls. There was enough clear ground for us to hang our

Steve with a black piranha.

hammocks easily, but we were far enough above the watermark that if there were to be a flash flood, all our gear would not be washed away! It was a long day travelling, but even so, we couldn't resist going out after dark and having our first look for a key Deadly beastie, the electric eel.

We've featured electric eels before, and I've been shocked by them several times. Once was here in Guyana, when a big eel blew me clear off my feet with a shock so powerful it would probably have killed me if I had been in the water. This made our goal here in jungle camp seem totally crazy. My intention was to use the clear water to our advantage, and try to actually film an eel underwater – a task that made me more than a little nervous!

The first thing we needed to do was to see if there were any eels there. To do that we had a kind of underwater aerial, which could pick up faint electric fields. Typically, the eels hunt at night in the pools underneath fast-flowing falls, so we put our kit into the water there. Straight away we got results: a faint ticking noise. This accelerated and got stronger, either as the unseen electric eel got closer, or as it stopped sensing the world around it and started sending out actual shocks, trying to deliver a fatal blast to its prey.

Then we saw our first eel, curling backwards out of a shallow pool under my torchlight. An electric eel is such a creepy sight, with its glazed eyes, purplish grey coloration and orange underbelly. This one was thick as my lower leg and well over a metre long. As the eel was there, relatively out in the open, I decided to go for broke and swooped in with a net. The last time I tried to catch an electric eel in a net, it took me two nights. This time I got it with a single scoop!

We tested the eel in a box full of water and even at rest it was ticking over with sixty or so volts. But when it got moving, it blasted away with over two hundred. Thankfully, we never got a full shock, which is six hundred and fifty volts, six times more potent than an American plug socket.

Next morning I was ready, mask and snorkel in hand, my heart racing. I did my best to run through all my checks, making sure the underwater camera was working properly, spitting into my mask to make sure it didn't steam up. Then I could wait no longer and dropped into the water upstream of the falls to drift down through the world of the most powerful electric creature on Earth – a fish that could stop a horse's heart with one blast. This brand new

Electric eel.

underwater vista took my breath away. The water was quite clear, with certainly three or four metres of visibility. Instantly a cloud of small brightly coloured fishes clustered around me, nibbling on my skin and biting on my moles and freckles, clearly believing them to be insects or ticks! Sometimes they'd nip particularly fiercely on a

Searching for an electric eel.

tender one, and I'd squeal with pain. The crew on the bank would jump out of their skins, thinking I'd been zapped by an eel!

In the heat of the day, the eels would be unlikely to be hunting but would be tangled up in the fallen tree roots that lined the riverbank. I poked around in the debris, as odd-looking catfish shuffled away at my approach, and colourful tetras and other aquarium beauties fluttered around me like butterflies. And then out of the gloom, a long snake-like shape emerged. I didn't need to worry about getting close to it – the eel came straight for me. My heart was in my mouth, as the fish swam right up into the camera lens. I've had this before from animals that can sense electrical pulses. Sharks will swim right into the camera, obviously stimulated by the weak electrical fields given off by the electronics. With the eel, though, it seemed to be even more of a fascination. The gruesome-looking creature repeatedly came to within a finger's breadth of the glass, before retreating, swimming just as well backwards as forwards. It was unutterably eerie.

After I'd found my first, the eels seemed to be everywhere. I found them swimming out in open water and could feel their sensing electric pulses vibrating right through my chest cavity. A very strange experience! By the

end of the day, I thought I had the measure of the eels and had perhaps built up a little too much confidence. This is precisely the time when accidents happen.

////////// **CLOSE SHAVE** \\\\\\\\\

I've found a deep green pool downstream of the camp, where at least six huge eels are swimming around, often in between sunken logs, occasionally in the open water. The fins that line their tails are pulsating in a way that is weirdly captivating. I'm trying my best to get a shot of this, but the light is low, and the camera keeps losing focus at the vital moment. So as I steady myself for a shot, I reach out to what I thought was a log to steady myself. It is as though I've stuck wet fingers in a toaster. The jolt blows all the way up my arm – I've clearly touched an eel that I hadn't seen, and it has given me a little warning blast. My fingers feel singed, as if I've stuck them on a hotplate. I'm also badly shaken up, and all of a sudden reminded of the potential danger of what I'm doing. Hauling myself back on the boat, I decide that the footage might not be perfect, but it is time to call it a day!

///////////////////////////////

Record-breaking arachnid

It was way back on series one of Deadly that we last featured the world's biggest spider: the goliath bird-eating spider, *Theraphosa blondii*. It was about time this huge beauty made a comeback. At our deep jungle camp, we sent the whole crew out working patterns around the tents, to see if we could find any sign of a burrow. The word came back quicker than anyone could have expected. There was a massive burrow of a bird eater no more than a minute's walk from camp! We waited till after dark, as this is when spiders wander out into the open, ready to sit in the mouth of their burrow to ambush their prey.

Steve with a goliath bird-eating spider.

I spend a lot of time trying to convince people not to be afraid of spiders, telling them that they are fascinating beasts that mean us no harm. I've also caught hundreds of tarantulas in the wild, and I've found that they all have their own personalities. Most are timid and will scamper for their burrows as soon as they are approached. Others can be flirty, responding to your tickles as if you are a potential mate.

Every once in a while you get a bitey one. This big girl was one of those. As I tried to coax her into my hands, she rose up and stabbed at me with her massive fangs. Tarantulas do not have potent venom, but the fangs are so long that the wound could be really painful. I have to admit to breaking out in a cold sweat as I tried to take her into my hand but finally managed it. She didn't bite, but she did flick the stinging hairs off her abdomen – something that these spiders do to defend themselves. Some went up my nose and started to itch like crazy. Others got into the skin of my forearms and itched so furiously that I couldn't sleep. They were still itching three days later!

BRAZIL

One question I am often asked is; 'Is there any animal that you just can't seem to find?' Well there is. It's the jaguar. I've spent literally months in the tropical rainforests of South and Central America solely bent on finding one of these rare and elusive spotted cats, but never seen so much as a track. There's a reason for that. Jaguars are rare, specialise in not being seen, are mostly nocturnal and, after decades of being hunted, they are understandably nervous of humans.

However, while filming the first series of Deadly in Brazil, I met a man who'd been working in a wetland area of Brazil called the Pantanal. He told me that jaguars were seen almost every day there, and that if we came out for a week at the right time of year we'd see one. Obviously I was sceptical, but the more we investigated, the more it seemed he might be telling the truth. Over the following five years we planned to go out, but something always got in the way. First I had a rock-climbing fall and broke my back. Then a big expedition looking for tigers went on right through the summer. Finally, though, on Pole to Pole we made our way to the Pantanal, at the exact right time of year. The challenge was on.

Spotty but never spotted

We were staying on a houseboat at the riverside. The jaguar were known to come to the river in the early morning to catch the breeze. We set out before sunrise every day, bleary-eyed and expectant. The first signs were fantastic. I asked our boat driver to pull up

Examining jaguar tracks.

at a sandy beach, and I jumped out to look for prints. What I found was a line of deep, deep cat tracks, fresh, perfect. Even better, alongside them was a line of much smaller, shallow cat tracks. Clearly the larger tracks belonged

to a female jaguar and she had a cub with her! We quickly set about putting half a dozen camera traps in likely spots, almost all of which had some jaguar tracks in evidence. But then the trail went cold. For three days we scoured the river, trawling up and down, and saw nothing at all. Well, that's not true. We saw thousands of crocodiles and the bird life was incredible. One evening, we heard some alarm calls from a capybara and pulled in our boat alongside, in case they were warning of the presence of a jaguar. Within minutes, fifteen other boats had pulled in too, thinking we had seen something. One nearby boat had some really moody tourists on board, who shouted at us for taking up the best spot in front of the jaguar that wasn't there! We sat and waited for two hours, but saw nothing.

On the penultimate night, we went back to check our camera traps. My heart leapt as I approached our main beach. There were clear tracks from a

Checking a camera trap.

jaguar, strolling past one of the cameras, then creeping up towards the tracks of a caiman. The tracks then clearly leapt forward and showed that the jaguar had dragged the caiman up the beach. We had caught a kill on our camera trap! I was going to be the owner of some of the finest footage ever shot! I checked the first trap. As I opened it, all the batteries fell out. They had been loose. The camera hadn't recorded anything. Then the second. It was corrupted, and had recorded nothing. The

> ## PORTRAIT OF A PREDATOR
> ### JAGUAR (*Panthera onca*)
> **Maximum size:**
> 158 kilograms; 2.4 metres long.
> **Range:**
> forest habitats across Central and South America.
> **Deadly fact:**
> the jaguars of the Pantanal specialise in killing caiman, biting clear through their heavy bony skulls.

third, surely this must have something? Well, nope. In fact it seemed to have missed the jaguar by a hair's breadth, and instead had loads of the shots of the vultures that must have swooped in to feed on what was left of the kill. We left with heavy hearts, feeling that the jaguar's position as Deadly nemesis was never going to be beaten.

The last day had an air of desperation about it. We got up when it was still dark and headed upriver. Everyone was stressed and irritable; the pressure was getting to us all. It was a tense steam upriver, coats pulled round our throats to abate the dawn chill, oblivious to the weak pink light reflecting off the water. It was still little more than half light, when we heard a capybara calling the alarm, then suddenly three of them leapt clear off the bank and into the river, like round furry Tom Daleys, splashing into the water in panic. There was no doubt they were responding to the presence of a predator.

Following pages: Steve close to a jaguar – at last.

Capybara on the riverbank.

Our senses keen, eyes sharp, we peered into the gloom of the gallery forest for the tell-tale sign of a speckled cat. Then Luke our second cameraman who was in the second boat barked into the radio, 'Jaguar!' We turned the boat and crept round the riverside, desperately hoping for a sighting. There it was! A female jaguar, slinking along the banks, then abruptly disappearing into the undergrowth. She was too quick for us to get a shot. We allowed ourselves to be carried by the current, floating downstream in the direction she had been moving. Our patience was rewarded, as she stepped from the shadows and lay down underneath a tree, then began grooming herself, licking each one of her curved sharp claws. She was breathtaking, and we had her all to ourselves for what seemed like an age. However, finally other boats started turning up, and not wanting to get in the way of their experience we reluctantly started the motor and set off.

When we arrived back at the houseboat for a much needed breakfast, the boat captain shouted out, 'A jaguar! Just downstream!' And there it was, this time a male and no more than two hundred metres away. There is no difficulty in distinguishing between male and female. While she is sleek and elegant, the male is much bigger, bulky and powerful. He looks as if he could take down a buffalo… which he probably could. Here at the riverside, the jaguars' main prey is caimans, which they kill with a bite clean through the bony skull. And then as we turned away and headed back to the boat, we saw YET another jaguar, this time a female, wandering through riverside rushes. Nothing in three days, then three in three hours. Quite a hit rate!

A female jaguar grooming herself.

Crafty caiman

The jaguar was a mighty tracking challenge, but our next Deadly contenders were impossible to avoid. They were everywhere! The Yacare caiman is one of the most numerous crocodilians on Earth, and in the Pantanal there are literally millions of them. If you go out at night and shine a flashlight through the local fishponds, thousands of fireflies appear to glow back at you.

Above and following pages: Yacare caiman.

In fact, this is eyeshine from the lurking crocs, waiting to munch down their fish dinners. The largest numbers are found around drying-out ponds, where fish are trapped together in artificially high concentrations. You could walk across the water on the caiman's backs there are so many of them. I sat by one of these pools with cameraman Mike for several hours, trying to catch the moment of strike. Mike was armed with the high-speed camera, which left me to take the main camera. He was very brave! None of the other cameramen would let me loose with that expensive bit of kit. However, I managed to get a few captures on camera, almost all in focus, and Mike (being a consummate pro) got some sensational shots of the caiman feeding in super slo mo. It was his first Deadly shoot, but will certainly not be his last! The next stop was to Deadly it all up, by getting into the water with the crocs.

CLOSE SHAVE

We've found a place where there is a shallow entry into the river. Unfortunately, the water is exceedingly murky, visibility close to zero. I wade into the water with my underwater camera, tiptoeing forward and expecting every step to land on the head of an angry crocodile! My nervousness is given cause when a good-sized caiman pops up no more than two metres away and makes a beeline straight for me. To distract it, our boatman and guide Ailton dangles a dead piranha on a line in front of me, tempting the caiman closer, but keeping his attention on the fish not on me. By now the croc is brushing my camera, and occasionally my fingertips. It takes every ounce of restraint in my body not to bump him away, but I know from experience this would be a bad idea. Crocs are well used to bumping into inanimate hard objects as they swim underwater and simply turn away from them. However, if something bumps into them with impetus it's usually prey, so their reaction is to lash out and bite.

Yacare caiman are not maneaters, they feed on fish. However, their sixty to eighty cone-shaped teeth are as long as my little finger and driven by a hefty bony jaw. The croc in front of me is bigger than I am and could do me a lot of damage. So I sit tight and let him make all the decisions. Thankfully, he just noses around my camera and munches down fish, all seen in close-up, and in focus (though that is probably more by luck than by judgement!).

Fishhook feet

As we returned from our jaguar spotting each evening, just as the light dropped too low for us to film, the surface of the river came alive with flapping, fluttering creatures that kept pace with us even at top speed. These were animals we've seen many times in Latin America, but never been able to film: fishing bats. They're one of the craziest, super-sensed creatures on Earth, but they only seem to be active for a few hours around dusk and they move really fast. While most bats feed on fruit or insects, these miraculous flappers snatch fish that are dozing just below the surface of the water, using echolocation to pinpoint the ripples that they create on the surface.

It was just after dark, and we were about to go out on a night hunt for wildlife. I was sitting in one of the small boats, waiting for the others to get their kit together, when I realised that the bats were flying quite close. As an experiment, I snatched a leaf from a nearby tree, tore off a piece and threw it down on to the water. BAM! A bat switched course in the blink of an eye, swooped down and caught the leaf as it hit the water. Incredible! I threw another leaf – BAM! Perfect! I tried this ten times, and it worked nine of those.

When the crew came down, I showed them my new trick and begged them to film it. However, the whole set-up, with lights and high-speed camera, would have taken hours, so we decided to leave it until the following evening and instead went out on a night drive. We found nothing at all. The next night we all got back to the boat, shattered after eighteen hours on the river, and set up to do the night filming with bats. We waited. And waited. Every night until then, the bats had been like a swarm of bees over the river, but not tonight. In fact, there were none at all. Disaster! We went farther out into the river, me armed with handfuls of leaves, and eventually a few bats turned up. I bundled up my first leaf and it crumbled into dust. Then the second. It cracked up into useless pieces.

Two hours later and we'd not even got close. Poor Mike had been sitting with the high-speed camera balanced on his lap, barely moving, focused on a tiny patch of light cast by my torch. I was doing my best to throw the tempting leaves into the pool of light, but I'd been bitten by a piranha during the day. It had taken off my fingertip and blood was leaking everywhere, all over the boat and the cameras. There were no bats, the leaf trick wasn't working. The exhausted, haggard crew members were looking at me with increasing frustration, and my usual confidence was starting to wane. High-speed cameras are temperamental at the best of times, and in normal conditions, I would expect to need ten attempts to get one good shot. We'd got none.

Then out of nowhere a flying beetle landed on my jumper. I plucked it off and tossed it into the light. A bat swooped sideways and snatched it from the water. 'FIRE, FIRE, FIRE!' I yelled, nearly toppling the boat over in my excitement. Mike looked up from his camera, and shrugged, as if to say; 'Maybe'. My heart sank, but we played the shot back just in case. It showed the

Fishing bat.

water looking like velvet, then the insect hit the water and ripples spread out smoothly in super slow mo, like the pressure wave from a vast volcano. And then from nowhere, a Dracula-like apparition appeared from the side of the shot. As it flew in, the claws dropped below it like grappling hooks, tracing the water, cutting a gutter through the velvet, before snatching up the beetle with unfathomable accuracy. It was perfect. It simply could not be improved upon. I know natural history camera people who could work a month to get a shot like that in carefully arranged and staged conditions. Mike achieved it in a tiny wobbling boat, holding the camera by hand, using the light of a hand torch, and with only one attempt. It was one of the greatest shooting achievements I've ever seen!

PATAGONIA

At the extreme south of the continent, Patagonia is paradise for adventurers and wildlife lovers alike. Its huge spiky mountain peaks and wind-lashed coastline were a taste of what we would experience as we continued south towards Antarctica. This would be our last stop in the Americas, so we needed something special. We had come here to find what is perhaps the premium predator on the planet: the only animal other than man known to kill great white sharks, a predator which will drown great whales or herd fish with great teamwork and organisation. It is an animal that in Patagonia more than anywhere else shows its complexity, intelligence and daring – the orca, sometimes known as the killer whale.

Blackfish

We made our way over several days to the Peninsula Valdez, hoping to see a unique hunting strategy, not known to occur anywhere else. The area is home to thousands of seals and therefore becomes the target for orca that want to make them lunch. A vast beach runs for many miles, with a flat reef out in front of it. As the tides come and go, they leave channels where the water goes from deep to shallow very quickly. The orca are only really interested in the young, inexperienced seals, and they splash in the surf, right on the beach. To catch them, the orca must power right up to them, in the process risking beaching themselves on the sand. It's one of the great spectacles in nature.

PORTRAIT OF A PREDATOR

KILLER WHALE/ORCA
(*Orcinus orca*)

Maximum size:
9.8 metres; 9,000 kilograms.

Range:
all oceans and major seas.

Deadly facts:
orca stick with their mums. The members of a pod are almost all related and kept in check by the matriarch, the senior female.

To film this though, we would need a phenomenal amount of luck. Our colleagues at the Natural History Unit had spent eight weeks here when they came for the same reason. We only had five days. It was entirely possible that the orca might not turn up at all in this time, and we would see nothing. It was one of the great gambles of the series. Our wait for the whales would not be easy. It was going to be very cold, occasionally very wet, and we were going to have to sit totally still, silent, and keeping a low profile so as not to spook the seals.

On the first day, it seemed that this may well have been a gamble too far. We sat on the beach for about ten hours in the sleet and driving rain, and the orca never showed. From where we were, we could see for several miles down the beach, so we would have been able to predict an attack hours before it happened. There was not even the possibility of success, which made for a thoroughly frustrating and even boring day.

On the following day, things began to hot up. At around mid-morning, we saw the distinctive silhouettes of orca dorsal fins way off in the distance. They coursed towards us, before circling around in front of the attack channel as if waiting for their chance. Unfortunately, the young seals were

Orca in the attack channel.

Top: Seals on the beach, watched by orca in the water.

Below: Orca surge in for the attack.

not playing in the surf, so they kept their distance. It is impossible to know how orca perceive where the seals are. The waves are crashing and they are submerged so they cannot possibly see their prey. The obvious answer would be echolocation, but orca have been proved to go silent as they swim into the attack channel, so it's unlikely to be that. But however they do it, the orca obviously know when there is no point in attacking, so keep their distance. As so often happens on Deadly, it was the last day before they made their move.

Again, it was mid-morning before anything started to happen. The orca came in from afar, led by a mature male with a vast scything dorsal fin that must have been as tall as I am. They loitered in the waves in front of the attack channel, and we waited, cameras poised. As we watched with baited breath,

The orca strikes.

a small party of young seals left their mother's sides and splashed down in the surf, crossing through the danger zone. The orca closed in, like impossibly sinister, dark, lurking submarines, locked on to their targets. There was a part of all of us that wanted to shout a warning, to call to the young seals and tell them of the horrific danger they were in. Seals splashed and orca surged in, but at the last minute they always turned away.

Finally, with the tide turning and time running out, a mother seal and her youngster splashed down in the waves. One of the mature female orca turned and headed straight for them. At the last stage she powered forward with extraordinary speed and force, lunging out of the water and up on to the sands. Her nose bumped the young seal, and it leapt forward. The mother reacted with lightning reflexes and incredible courage, putting her own body between her youngster and the huge predator. The hunt had failed by millimetres.

Now grounded on the sand, the orca flexed her body, flapping her tail up and down and see-sawing her huge heavy body to bounce herself back into the surf. Though we hadn't managed to capture a successful hunt on camera, we all felt we could return home happy. The orca had attacked, and the lucky seal had escaped. It seemed the right result!

A grounded orca bounces herself back into the water.

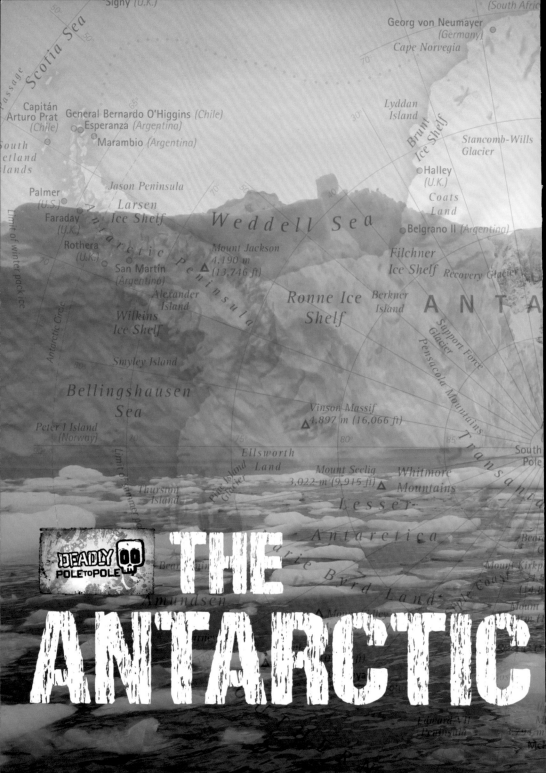

The Antarctic Circle includes all the area south of 60 degrees latitude. Antarctica is a place of extremes. It is the coldest continent on Earth, with a record low temperature of –94.7 degrees centigrade. It is also the windiest. Cape Denison has had a weather station since the early 1900s and they have hurricane force winds about every three days. The average wind speed is a severe gale, force nine on the Beaufort scale. Even though Mount Vinson at 4,897 metres is the biggest single mountain, most of the landmass is over 1,000 metres so it is the highest continent on average. It is also the most remote, least inhabited and wildest, and finally it is the driest. In parts of the interior the air is too cold to hold water and there is never any precipitation of any kind – no snow or rain. In winter the continent is doubled in size by growing pack ice. The ice in Antarctica may lock up 75 per cent of the world's freshwater, and over 98 per cent of the continent is permanently covered with snow, even in mid-summer.

FALKLAND ISLANDS

We spent much of our time in the sub-Antarctic islands of the Falklands and South Georgia. These are at relatively low latitudes, but the conditions created by the weather systems and ocean currents that swirl around Antarctica make them challenging and often inhospitable places.

The Falklands is stranded where the cold currents from Antarctic waters swirl into the warmer South Atlantic. This mixing brings nutrients to the surface and creates a phantasm of marine life. The islands are pretty barren – it's too windy for any trees, and only very low-lying vegetation can grow. In this cruel and exposed world, the islands are like arks, their tussock grasses and beaches offering shelter and refuge for wildlife. At certain times of year, any land near the coast is overflowing with birds.

From the Falklands to Antarctica we were breaking new ground for Deadly. No one on the team had done any of this before, and everything we were seeing was new. There was a wonderful fresh excitement in the air, even after more than a year on the road.

Bouncy birds

Penguins were our constant companions from the Falklands all the way
south. There are seventeen different species (not all of which live in
Antarctica) and they are very special birds indeed. The body shape is dumpy
and rounded in profile, more like something you'd expect to see on a marine
mammal like a seal than a bird. The wings have lost their function in getting
airborne and instead act like flippers, driving the bird along at great speed
in the water. Losing the ability to fly has freed penguins from the need to
be super-lightweight. While flying birds have bones with lots of air space
inside, and minimal amounts of body fat, penguins lay down huge layers of
blubber. This fatty layer provides insulation in the chilly waters and also gives
the birds an energy store if they have go for long periods without food – a
certainty in this sub-polar world.

Rockhopper penguins are robust little devils and well-named. They spend
most of the year in waters to the north of the Falklands, hunting for squid,
small fish and krill, but they come to land to breed, lay their eggs and raise
their young. The breeding colonies are located on precipitous slopes, and to
get up to them, the rockhoppers 'boing' their way upwards, even on the most
vertical of cliff faces. If they slip, they bounce their way down like a half-
deflated rugby ball.

The first part of filming them
was a doddle. We simply
wandered up to the colony and
sat within metres as they went
about their business, hopping up
and down from the coast to feed
their youngsters. The second bit
was harder. I really wanted to
see them at their lethal best,
and that would mean getting
wet. I sat in the surf by one of

Above and following pages:
Rockhopper penguins.

the colonies, watching as they zipped through the waves. However, they clearly thought that I looked a bit too much like a predatory leopard seal and avoided me like the plague. I sat there in the chill getting smashed by the spray for two hours until I couldn't talk cos my face was numb, but they didn't come even close.

Southern sea lions were next. They were to prove quite a challenge. Their main colony was on an uninhabited rocky hummock called Kidney Island. As we arrived in our boat, several heads popped up nearby. The sea lions seemed to be intrigued. We kitted up as quickly as we could and dropped into the water, but the sea lions were in among the densest kelp forest I have ever seen. We couldn't get near them, and they were showing no signs of approaching us underwater. The first dive was wasted. We saw nothing at all.

Expedition planning.

We decided to switch location and moved to a place where we could see more sea lions playing around. This lot, though, were close to some big rocks, and the swell was crashing in, causing a veritable whirlpool. Our scuba kit made us slow and sluggish, vulnerable underwater. As we approached, picking our way through the kelp forest, I got tangled up over and over again and I was burning air and energy even getting close. Then we saw our first flash of sea lion flipper. Excited, I finned towards it, Johnny in hot pursuit. This got us to an area with a rocky outcrop between me and the camera boat. They can talk to us underwater through a radio transmission system, but if the way is blocked, we can't communicate. If I had been able to hear, I would have heard them yelling to be careful of the current and the rocks. Instead I found out the hard way.

Suddenly, I was being tumbled around, as if I'd been caught in a washing machine on spin cycle. Johnny fared even worse, as he had the big camera to contend with. I grabbed for the kelp, taking a hold and steadying myself. As we embarrassed ourselves, being thrashed around in the waves, the sea lions danced and pirouetted nearby seeming to mock our clumsiness. I have never felt quite so helpless and hopeless underwater!

One of the great dramas of filming at the beach where the rockhoppers nested, was seeing black and white Comerson's dolphins. They were surfing in the waves, then coasting in to the beaches, slicing their way to within metres of land. I'd never seen this small and comely species of dolphin before, and it is without doubt one of the most beautiful. And what a welcome surprise to spot yet another unseen species riding in the bow wave at the front of our boat. These were Peale's dolphins, a little larger than the Comerson's, but with a similar porpoise-like shape and also bearing stark grey, black and white colours. Most remarkable, was the fact that the dolphins rode our bow wave for at least half an hour, then as we all disembarked to go ashore and film the sea lions, they stuck around our boat for at least another hour. It was clear they were in playful spirits.

Peale's dolphin.

When we returned and found them still around, the temptation was just to jump over the side and join them, but we knew our captain was anxious that a storm might be approaching, and we needed to head to port. Expecting a 'No', I tentatively asked if we might have another hour. The captain looked up at the skies, then at the waters and the dolphins splashing around, obviously calling out, 'Come and play with us!' He smiled and nodded his head.

Cameraman Johnny and I had only our dry suits, which we use for diving in these icy waters. They were too buoyant to allow us to dive alongside the dolphins, or to swim much, but it didn't matter. Time and again, the Peale's dolphins surged towards us then banked away at the last second, clearly showing off their skills. It was an exhilarating experience and our hour was over all too soon.

Due south

The adventure was only just beginning. I have dreamed about heading down the southern continent since I was a small boy, and yet have never been able to make it happen. Finally, though, my dreams were about to come true. However, there is many a slip twixt cup and lip, and there was a vast expanse of ocean to cover before we arrived at our destination. We would be at sea for over a month, in the most notorious waters on the planet. It was to be the biggest sea journey that any of the crew had undertaken. We had all been thoroughly panicked beforehand, and despite the fact that I've never been seasick, I'd gone to the doctors to get the strongest seasickness medication available, as I was expecting to get ill at some point. This seemed even more likely when we saw our boat, the *Hans Hansell*, for the first time. She was just over twenty metres in length and, though a sturdy-looking vessel, seemed very small to be trusting ourselves to, afloat on the wildest seas.

The first night all our worst fears were realised. The boat pitched and rolled so violently that anything that wasn't tied down was thrown around the cabin. Drawers and doors slammed like cannon-fire. I managed to crawl across the floor in order to put boards into the side of my bunk and stuff either side with bags, cushions, clothing, anything I could find to avoid being thrown out of bed with every wave.

Nobody slept a wink, and just after sunrise I decided to get up and make a cup of tea. After half an hour being thrown around the galley, and actually quite hurting myself, I gave up and went back to bed. The idea of going through this for over a month was simply unthinkable.

But then everything changed. As the day wore on the sun came out and the west winds fell neatly behind us. The swell dropped and the boat was no longer all over the place. I didn't take any more seasickness pills and even managed to go out on deck and do some Backshall's bootcamp! I did some chin-ups while being thrown around side to side, then press-ups lashed by occasional wave spray! That night I slept like a lullabied baby, gently swaying in my maritime bassinet.

Day three at sea, and we had covered 800 of the 1,600 kilometres to our destination of South Georgia. Our researcher, though, was not doing so well. She was knocked out cold by the seasickness patches she used, and her eyes could not focus on close objects. She turned into a total zombie and couldn't get out of bed at all. The sea was still wobbly enough to be confining most of the team to bunks, but I felt like a million dollars. I was sure I'd get my comeuppance for being so smug at some stage on the trip, but I had a wonderful day, mostly sitting writing, or out on deck watching the birds.

Ocean wanderer
Bird watching here in the Southern Ocean is not like it is in most other places. There might not be another boat for 150 kilometres, so you become the focal point for everything that flies. This is for several reasons. First, ships at sea often tip their refuse overboard, and much of it is edible. Second, the passage of the boat stirs up the ocean and may bring fish, squid and other nutrients to the surface. Third, the wind driven over the boat creates vortexes that bring lift to the wings of our most aerial birds. With my bird guide in one hand and binoculars in the other, I spotted thirty species that day, from the tiny storm petrels that fly like bats and pitter-patter on the sea surface to draw small creatures up to the surface, to the vast albatross.

There is a solitary majesty to the wandering albatross that makes me melancholy. It cruises over the waves, one wing tip coursing the surface of the water like a sword, and travels for many days without a wing beat. It is the largest flying bird alive today, but also surely one of the most lonesome.

For the first four years of an albatross's life, it never comes to land but just scours the deep blackness of the open sea in search of food. It will not find a mate and breed successfully until it is about nine years old on average. After that, it returns to the same spot every two years, where it meets the lover it hasn't seen for so long. They perform a duet, dancing together to reaffirm their love before they mate.

However, in this human age of long-lining, a commercial fishing technique in which long lines are placed in the sea with large numbers of baited hooks, many albatross, particularly females, are being tugged underwater by

Wandering albatross on Bird Island.

Black-browed albatross.

fishermen's hooks and drowned, never to return. Imagine the trauma of being out at sea for two years, only to return to your nest and find your partner doesn't arrive. It's too tempting to impose human emotions on animals, but for me, the wandering albatross seems the most sorrowful of birds, an emperor of impossibly regal bearing, condemned to live a lonely life.

Bird Island
Bird Island is located at the far northwest apex of South Georgia and is the first place the west winds hit after they have whipped around Antarctica. The island is eternally lashed by brutal winds, which birds like the albatross adore. It was first discovered by Captain James Cook on the journeys of the ship *Resolution* in 1775. He apparently stated that, 'the inner parts of the country were not less savage and horrible… not a tree or shrub was to be seen, not even big enough to make a toothpick.' Cook was definitely not a fan. He had been hoping to discover the great southern continent of Antarctica and as he rounded the headlands at the southernmost point, realising how far off he was, named it Cape Disappointment. We arrived delighted to see land after our five days of vomit-inducing rolling at sea.

We were also to be blown away by the sheer amount of life that gives the place its name. At certain times of year there is a greater concentration of birds and seals here than on any other place on Earth.

Giant wave wanderer

We were to have our iconic encounter with the wandering albatross on the slopes of Bird Island, where they come ashore to breed. One of the best-known wildlife filming images of all time is Sir David Attenborough himself, crouched behind two wandering albatross as they display to each other, with the snow-capped peaks of South Georgia in the background. We came back to the very spot and recreated the sequence ourselves. Admittedly it wasn't anything like as perfect – they probably had weeks to get it right, we only had a few hours. I had to sprint over every time we saw two birds flirting, sit behind them and just blag it.

An albatross pair performing their elegant duet.

Nothing can prepare you for seeing a wandering albatross on land. I've seen hundreds on the wing, and they look big, but the first time you see one sitting on the nest, it takes your breath away. A mature male bird standing comes up to your chest, its body at least as large as a mute swan. When it spreads its wings it makes you gasp. People say that they can measure as much as 4.2 metres, a fact that I was a little sceptical about. But we measured the wings of a female (the males are bigger) of unremarkable size and with incomplete primaries, and they were 3.5 metres. I have no doubt 4.2 metres is possible – that's as long as two second-row rugby forwards lying head to head.

PORTRAIT OF A PREDATOR

WANDERING ALBATROSS
(Diomedea exulans)

Maximum size:
wingspan 3.63 metres (confirmed record); 11.5 kilograms.

Range:
mostly southern oceans, can circumnavigate the planet in a month.

Deadly fact:
the shoulder joint has a unique arrangement that locks in place when the wings are extended. It allows the bird to glide and soar with no expenditure of energy.

The song and dance routine they run through is so beautiful that a description in words seems pointless, but I'll try. First, the male approaches, head down, humpbacked, waddling from side to side with an exaggerated swagger. The female comes to meet him and they both spread their wings wide (usually clouting me in the face in the process). Then the male throws his head back, huge bill pointing skywards, before sounding a far-reaching clarion call to the wind. They touch each other's bills tenderly, preen each other, then begin again. It is a duet any prima ballerina would appreciate.

Antarctic fur seals

Another animal occurs here in far greater numbers than the albatross, littering the beaches in hundreds of thousands. The Antarctic fur seal was once hunted to the edge of extinction for its dense fur coat, but has bounced back in considerable style. As you walk along the beaches, the seals gaze with their dark puppy-dog eyes, then lunge towards you roaring, baring their teeth and making to bite. They need to be nudged away firmly with a stick or your boot or they will plunge their teeth into your bottom.

As always though, these creatures are not at their best on land, so we needed to get shots of them underwater. We found a bay that was reasonably sheltered, and Johnny the cameraman and I dropped over the side. Within seconds, we were mobbed. The females were the first to pay us a visit, swarming all over us, travelling at immense speed. Then the pups nosed right into the lens, staring at us with wondering soulful eyes. The skills they were showing off to us were exactly the same techniques they would need to snaffle down their prey. And while it is mostly fish, fur seals have also been witnessed attacking and killing the penguins that share their beaches.

Antarctic fur seal.

We left the water chilled to the bone and went straight to bed in our cabins, where we lay shivering under our duvets for three or four hours before we felt warm again. The water here is a balmy two degrees – in Antarctica where we were heading it would be 1.8 degrees below freezing. I wasn't sure I was looking forward to it!

Vulture of the south

As with anywhere you find this much life, there is also an unfortunate amount of death. On a bad year, only one in ten of the seal pups make it to adulthood. Many of those that don't survive die right here on these beaches,

Brown skuas and giant petrels scavenge a fur seal carcass.

and something has to clear up the mess. This far south there are very few insects to do the job, and no vultures either, but there are several birds that tackle the task more than adequately. The Antarctic skua is perhaps the most prominent. We'd met its relative the Arctic skua all the way up in Svalbard at the start of our journey, harassing reindeer and dive-bombing me. These birds flock to a carcass like a murder of crows. They're intelligent, and you can see them looking at you and trying to figure out if you might have anything on you they could eat or steal.

The same can't be said of the next bird that arrives at a carcass, the giant petrel. It is much, much bigger and looks like a waddling dinosaur, with a huge beak straddled with two tube nostrils. These give the bird a keen sense of smell and also the ability to shed the excess salt it gets from its food and seawater. Giant petrels plunge their heads into carcasses, emerging besmeared with blood and goo. Though they are somewhat grim, I took to them instantly. They seemed to have a great deal of character and are very important, ensuring the beaches are not clogged with rotting bodies.

SOUTH GEORGIA

South Georgia looks rather as if the gods had taken a slice of snow-capped mountain range and simply dropped it into the Southern Ocean. The islands have no near neighbours – Antarctica and South America are about 1,600 kilometres away. There is no permanent population, no towns other than scientific research stations, but this is one of the greatest places for wildlife on the whole planet.

The boat sailed overnight from Bird Island and landed at Grytviken. This was a sad and strange place. Grytviken was a bustling whaling port from 1904 to 1964, and part of one of the world's biggest whaling industries. Here they caught many of the great whales we have featured on Deadly, including blue whales, sperm, fin and humpbacks. About 175,000 were killed in these waters, 1.4 million in the Southern Oceans as a whole. The reason the operations ended in the sixties was that there simply were no whales left to catch. Grytviken has been left as a rusting monument to those terrible times. Here you can see the vast melting pots, where the whale oils were rendered down to make margarine and lubricants. The bones were ground and used as fertiliser.

One simple sign really struck home. It said that thirty whales could be processed here in a day, and the largest was a single female who was thirty-four metres long and getting on for two hundred tonnes in weight. Though I wasn't aware of it, I have known about her for many years and quoted her

Above and following pages: Abandoned whaling station at Grytviken.

vital statistics in dozens of lectures and programmes, for one simple reason. She was the biggest animal that has ever been seen on our planet, more massive than any of the known dinosaurs. And she was killed here in 1912 to be made into margarine and bonemeal.

Whale numbers have never recovered in South Georgia. The great whales take many years to reach maturity and to breed. They may never recover. Grytviken was to me a reminder of human greed, of excess and short-sightedness. I felt sadder there than anywhere on this whole expedition.

Grytviken is also home to the grave of Sir Ernest Shackleton. After British naturalist and explorer Alfred Russel Wallace, he is my greatest hero in history and seeing his simple monument, pointing south towards the Pole he so coveted, was a surprisingly emotional moment for me. I had it to myself for

about fifteen minutes. It's probably the closest I've come in my adult life to prayer and I felt genuinely annoyed when the others turned up, laughing and taking photos. I'm not saying this to blame anyone. It doesn't make any sense to be moved by the grave of someone who's been dead for a century and you never knew. Perhaps the whole whaling thing had me emotional already, I don't know. All I do know, is that whenever I've felt as if things have been hard on an expedition in the past, I've thought back to Shackleton, to what he did and achieved, in order to give myself some perspective, get some backbone and man the hell up! It was important to me. I was glad to have come.

All of this is framed by a backdrop of quite ludicrous beauty. The highest peaks are 3,000 metres, and glaciers calve icebergs into the seas around us. It was, though, the windiest place I have ever been. The wind could drive you insane: gale force almost constantly as the west winds and roaring forties rage around Antarctica, battering these rocky islands into submission. It feels like the end of the Earth. We wrapped ourselves in multiple layers and huge coats, yet still had to eat enormous amounts of stodgy food just to keep our engines going!

Imperial diver

Our next stop was one of the great natural wonders of the world. The last census at St Andrew's Bay recorded 150,000 breeding pairs of king penguins. That was thirty years ago, and most observers believe numbers have more than doubled since then to well over half a million birds. It was totally overwhelming. As far as the eye could see along the beaches, kings stood like glorious gaudy bowling pins. When we approached, they would waddle up to us, extending their necks to give us a good look. While all penguin colonies are noisy, they normally give you earache. Here, though, it was a bit like standing among the horn section of a huge orchestra, constantly sounding off with beautiful bugling calls. The birds were surrounded by blue glaciers and craggy summits. Everywhere you looked was a National Geographic front cover waiting to be snapped. After a while I simply gave up taking photos, as my limited skills could not do the place justice.

Each bird is a marvel of evolution. Many millions of years ago, the penguin's ancestor would have been a flying seabird. Its flying wings would have been a considerable hindrance, though, for diving. (The wandering albatross with its vast wingspan cannot dive at all, and can only duck its head underwater.) Gradually, over millennia, the bird's wings shortened and stiffened. The joints inside the wings fused at the elbow and wrist, and the bones flattened and became stout and hefty. The wings became paddles, more like a seal's front flippers. Evolution may have appeared to go backwards, but in losing their power of flight, penguins have been freed to become the greatest swimmers and divers of all the 10,000 or so species of bird.

Kings are also the most beautiful of all penguins. They have an ivory-white belly and silver-grey back. This is the simple countershading camouflage shared by most marine predators – seen from below their belly blends into the white sky, while seen from above the dark back disappears into the blue of the deep. The head, which sticks up out of the water as the bird swims at the surface, is flamboyantly coloured, with a golden chest, ink-black face and spoon of orange about the ear patch. We'd seen a few individuals over the previous weeks and just sat and stared at their beauty. To see half a million in one place was sensory overload.

As with all marine mammals, reptiles or birds that come ashore to breed, penguins are mostly adapted to a life at sea, and the trade-off is that they're clumsy on land. However, we thought we had no chance of seeing

Right and following pages:
King penguins.

them at their deadly best underwater. The waters around their beaches are inevitably cloudy with glacial silt and the droppings of a hundred thousand bird bottoms. Or so we thought. Instead we woke to a wondrous surprise: our boat was surrounded by thousands of king penguins and the visibility was pretty good. We leapt out of bed in total panic. It was possible the penguins were heading out to feed. We thundered around the boat, yelling, 'Where's

Steve watches king penguins heading for the feeding grounds.

my mask?', and 'Is the underwater camera ready?', desperately trying to be in the water before the birds left us. Apologies for curtness could be made later; without an ounce of hyperbole this was the chance of a lifetime.

When we dropped into the water, we were greeted by a sublime sight. The penguins were fizzing past us like birdy bullets, trailing quicksilver bubbles behind them. Some came right up to the camera and pecked at the lens,

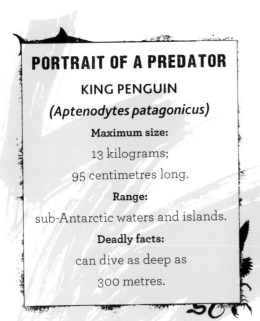

PORTRAIT OF A PREDATOR

KING PENGUIN

(Aptenodytes patagonicus)

Maximum size:

13 kilograms;

95 centimetres long.

Range:

sub-Antarctic waters and islands.

Deadly facts:

can dive as deep as

300 metres.

obviously intrigued about what it was. And no wonder. According to our captain Dion (the only person who has ever been born on South Georgia and grew up on a small yacht around these islands), nobody had ever dived with king penguins there. For the entire dive, we had at least forty in sight, the maelstrom of birds around the boat numbered thousands.

But after an hour's dive, I left the water furious with myself. In my urgency to get in, I had not taken enough weight and had struggled with buoyancy. Trying to battle the current in blue water, stay in front of Johnny's lens at the exact right distance, flush my mask, film with my underwater camera, deliver meaningful and relevant pieces to camera, while not swimming, moving or blowing out any bubbles (which scared off the penguins) all at the same time had proved too much for me. I'd been all over the place. In the rush, I had also only been able to find my liner gloves, so my fingers were frozen dead (excruciating as they warmed up again). It felt as if I had let everyone down, dropping the ball on a filming experience we could never repeat.

King penguins.

Trying not to show my disappointment, I reviewed the footage. Johnny had done an amazing job (as always). The penguins were flitting around me, always in shot, and it looked extraordinary. I went to bed overcome with relief and adrenalin, then slept for much of the rest of the day.

It was hard to leave South Georgia, particularly with the rafts of penguins still whirling around our boat. It is a place of ludicrous wildness and beauty, where as a human being you feel very small and exposed. I treasure places like this beyond all others, places where the modern world seems very far away. The wildlife had been far beyond my dreams, and at times it was difficult to find words to express quite how overwhelming it all was. Both the albatross and king penguins left me and a few other members of the crew a bit emotional, even teary. However, this was just the start of the adventure. From here, it was six days at sea until we reached our final destination: Antarctica.

South

It's difficult to express quite how much Antarctica means to me. Ever since I was a small boy, it has seemed to me the most wild, beguiling and intoxicating place on Earth. During my fifteen years in television, and the three before that as a travel writer, I have visited more than a hundred countries, been to all the places I have dreamed of and to every continent… except Antarctica. It is the last big tick on my life list. I've tried over and again to get there, but it has always been too expensive or logistically difficult. It was the whole reason I came up with Deadly Pole to Pole, and through all the trials, heartache and high times of this last thirteen months on the road, this has been my goal, the reason for it all. I have never been so excited to visit a place, ever.

Today, Antarctica has several scientific bases, most of which have at least a few people staying there, even through the constant dark of winter. It remains, however, without government, though under the agreement of many nations to the Antarctic treaty, which includes the following: Recognising that it is in the interest of all mankind that Antarctica shall continue for ever to be used for peaceful purposes and shall not become the scene or object of international discord.

To get to Antarctica, we have to cross another 1,600 kilometres of sea heading through the notorious Drake Passage. Dion looked at the weather reports with concern writ across his face. 'Galeforce winds and swell coming across us the whole way. I hope you're all ready for hell,' he said. And this is the man who summed up our first night being smashed about on the *Hans Hansell* as 'better than average'.

The first day and night were the worst I have ever experienced at sea. There was no sickness, just violence. It was impossible to get around the boat. One lunge threw you across the room and slammed you into the wall, as if you had been tossed by a raging elephant. Just trying to go to the toilet felt like a near-death experience.

After several days of this pounding, we were all beaten and battered. On the final night there was a force ten storm, with winds whipping the huge waves into prancing white ponies. At one stage during the night a wave broke clear over the top of the boat.

Day six since leaving South Georgia thankfully dawned on calmer seas. And as we came up to the bridge to admire our first big iceberg, we were rewarded with an even more welcome sight. In the slush of broken ice around its blue towers, three humpback whales were circling. They skyhopped to the surface, giving us a good look, then cruised alongside our boat, mere metres away.

A majestic Antarctic landscape.

THE ANTARCTIC PENINSULA

The South Pole was claimed in December 14, 1911 by Norwegian Roald Amundsen, a remarkable professional adventurer who had already attempted the North Pole and succeeded in travelling through the fabled Northwest Passage. His era is known also for the expeditions of Shackleton and Scott, both fantastically heroic and stoic but ultimately ill-fated, ending in courage and disaster.

Much of Antarctica remains unexplored even now. To penetrate far into the interior would take months and, more importantly, we would not find any animals. Instead, we concentrated our efforts on the long tongue of islands that point from the mighty southern continent, towards the base of South America. Much of the land and islands are permanently frozen into vast ice sheets and in the winter, the whole area is sealed with pack ice, whose growth effectively doubles the size of Antarctica.

Life here is dependent on Antarctic krill, small shrimp-like crustaceans that occur here in swarms of extraordinary density and size. It is probable that there is a greater mass of krill than of any other creature on Earth. One swarm seen off Elephant Island in 1981 was estimated to be 453 square kilometres in size, and contained 2.2 million tonnes of krill.

Weddell seals

Weddells are the most southerly breeding of all mammals and some of the greatest divers of all seals. Admittedly, they can be outdone by elephant seals, but those are leviathans, the size of small whales, and much of their diving ability is down to storing oxygen in their vast bulk.

Weddell seals have extraordinary physiological adaptations that enable them to dive to great depths in search of their prime prey, Antarctic cod. For instance, most mammals have thirteen sets of ribs, but Weddell seals have fifteen, to allow for larger lung space. They have a higher quality and quantity of blood – sixty per cent more than a human – and more of the oxygen-carrying molecule haemoglobin than we do. This enables them to carry nearly six times more oxygen in their blood than we can. Their muscles are even more well-adapted, capable of storing ten times more oxygen than a human of the same size. The muscles are so deeply red that they appear black. In deep dives, a Weddell's heart rate drops seventy-five per cent and it can stay down at 600 metres for an hour.

Sea spider

Diving in Antarctica is an adventure in itself. It takes a good deal of commitment to plunge into water under huge bobbing chunks of ice. The water is below freezing. In fact, it can reach minus 1.8 degrees centigrade, as the saltiness stops it turning solid at zero degrees. We were diving in a stunning cove called Paradise Bay, an amphitheatre of towering

Weddell seal.

mountains, with deep blue and white glaciers looking like petticoats around their flanks. The wind was racing, and we were all brutally chilled even before we got into the water.

Just seconds after Johnny and safety diver Terri had dropped in, dive supervisor Josh held up his hand to stop me going over the side of the Zodiac. 'I don't like the look of that berg,' he said, pointing to a huge glowing blue blob that was bearing down on us. He paused for a minute, then got on the underwater comms unit. 'Divers, abort, repeat abort dive, get to the surface as soon as possible.' Johnny and Terri were tugged on board, and we gunned the engine to move us away, mere minutes before the berg swept right through where we'd been.

Once we'd found ourselves a safer spot, we dropped down to twenty-one metres, where the visibility was good and clear. I searched among the fronds of seaweed for my prize – a sea spider. There are around 1,300 known species of sea spider, they have eight legs, four simple eyes on a turret and are vaguely similar to an underwater daddy-long-legs, though they are not true spiders. Instead they are more closely related to the prehistoric horseshoe crabs and a real oddity. They have no lungs or gills but absorb oxygen through their exoskeletons, effectively never taking a breath in their lives. Their jaws are very different to those of spiders or crabs, which have munching crunching mashing mouthparts. Instead, the sea spider has a beak-like proboscis which is much more like the rostrum (piercing mouthparts) you see on true bugs like assassin bugs, and works in the same way. The sea spider stabs this proboscis into soft-bodied prey like worms, sponges and sea anemones. Then it injects a digestive enzyme, which turns the prey into soup that can be sucked up. It walks backwards, but incredibly slowly, those spindly limbs not being much use for fast motion. When it's breeding time, the males carry their fertilised eggs around in a kind of frothy globular cluster.

Giant isopod
My last find beneath the bergs at Paradise Bay was a giant isopod, an odd beast which kind of looks like an oversized sea cockroach. In very cold waters many organisms grow more slowly than they do elsewhere and have slower metabolisms. In some cases they can also reach larger sizes. The giant

Steve holds a giant isopod.

isopods are just one example of this. Essentially they are big marine woodlice, primitive creatures probably most closely related to the horseshoe crabs. In Antarctica they are predominantly scavengers. Any carcass of a seal or whale that sinks to the bottom will soon be swarmed by these grotesque, alien-looking bugs. If they feel at all threatened, they put one pair of legs up into the water, perhaps brandishing these spikes as protection, or using them as a tactile device for sensing what's going on around them.

Leopard seal

In the shallow waters close to the penguin colonies, one mighty creature rules through brutal terror. It is a sinuous, long-necked, massive mammalian predator which skins penguins and smaller seals alive. This is the leopard seal, my greatest remaining underwater filming ambition and the main focus for our Antarctica programme.

Gentoo penguins.

For the first time we rose to blue skies, aquamarine and cobalt icebergs bobbing ominously in the glassy flat seas. Behind them were unclimbed mountains that enticed me, and glaciers of a size and scale unmatched by anything else on the planet. It was one of the most beautiful sights I've ever seen. Our first night we dropped anchor close to a gentoo penguin colony. The gentoos are the third largest species of penguin. They're adorable dumpy waddling wonders on land, but transformed underwater. Probably the fastest species of penguin, they porpoise enthusiastically as they thunder towards the colony. And for good reason; in the shallows lurked an animal of unimaginable ferocity. An animal that can shake them so hard it literally throws them out of their skins.

Chugging slowly between the bergs near shore, I heard the seal before I saw it: a dramatic expulsion of air that reverberated round the bergs like a loudspeaker, through nostrils that are usually clenched tight to keep the water out. And then it broke the surface, more like a crocodile than any seal I've ever seen. I had played this moment through in my mind a hundred times and fully expected the leopard seal to be large and scary. But even so, it took my breath away. It was as long as our Zodiac and still seemed to have a head too big for its body. It swam alongside us, then turned and swam at, then under the boat. With one huge bow wave, telling of the animal's bulk and power, it was gone. The encounter lasted only seconds, but left me in a cold sweat, heart pounding. Having dived with big crocodiles, hippos and out of the cage with every dangerous shark, I know a thing or two about scary aquatic predators, but there was something especially chilling about this one. It is a deeply sinister animal, almost seeming to wear a horror film smile, big eyes always sizing you up, and just enormous! There have been several attacks on humans, at least one of which was fatal. Our first sighting was a superb start, but ensured I didn't sleep well that night.

Up on the deck of the boat, we took a look at a leopard seal skull. You can learn an enormous amount about animals by looking at their skulls and teeth. It's something I particularly love to do with seals and sea lions, though, because they are animals that humans always, always underestimate. When

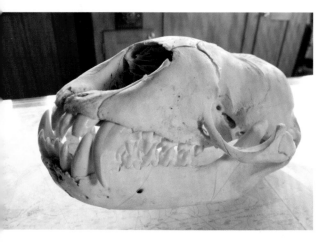

Leopard seal skull.

we hear sea lion, we think of the friendly comedy animals that turn up in aquarium side shows, but when you look at the skull of a big sea lion (or God forbid an elephant seal) it makes you gulp. If you didn't know what animal it was from, you would guess at an extinct sabre-toothed cat. The biggest grizzly or polar bear is eclipsed by a big sea lion skull, which has bigger canine killing teeth and looks just plain horrifying. The leopard seal skull is another level again. It, too, has huge canines, but it also has jagged tricuspid (three-cusped) teeth, farther back down the jaw, which can be used for sieving krill from the water. Its diet is probably fifty per cent krill, twenty per cent penguins and fifteen per cent seals, in addition to other seabirds, fish, squid and even whale carcasses. One adult, however, was found with sixteen adult penguins in its stomach, and six seals that were studied at length caught an average of eight penguins a day!

PORTRAIT OF A PREDATOR
LEOPARD SEAL
(Hydrurga leptonyx)
Maximum size:
600 kilograms;
over 4 metres long.
Range:
Antarctic ice shelf and occasional vagrants farther north.
Speed:
unknown, but considerable; can jump 2 metres out of the water on to bergs, travelling at 6 metres a second.
Deadly fact:
the only seal species that relies on warm-blooded prey.

Next day, we went ashore to get some footage of the gentoos. As soon as we got to land, a leopard seal came out of nowhere and buzzed our boat. We stood and waited and within minutes, it also made a lunge for a penguin, driving the water aside and getting ever so close to making a kill. Soon it disappeared, but we saw a long lithe shape lying on a low flat iceberg, what's known as a 'growler'. We squinted through our bins and clearly it had to be a leopard seal. Again, we took the Zodiac over to the berg for a closer look. This particular seal was sleeping and could not have been less interested in us. We got to the point where our boat was bumping the berg, and it didn't even budge. It was a massive gamble, but I decided we should try to dive with it.

Above: Filming a leopard seal sleeping on ice.
Previous pages: Leopard seal under water.

Everyone kitted up in a hurry, and got back into the Zodiac, hearts pounding. Up on deck, Dion the captain spotted with binoculars and gave us directions towards the seal. It was lying in the water alongside a glorious jade berg, coming to the surface like a crocodile does, with minimum exposure, just its nostrils and eyes showing. We could not put it off any longer. Dropping over the side, my breathing rate went through the roof. I battled to relax. 'Come on Backshall, calm down, it's just a seal,' I told myself. I looked down into my underwater camera and found it had a technical fault. It was stuck in autofocus and the image wouldn't sharpen. I frantically jabbed away at the controls, trying to get it working, knowing the seal could come out of the gloom at any second. In retrospect, this was the best thing that could have happened, helping me to focus on a task other than what was ahead.

But then she came out of the green water. I say she, because the largest animals are females, potentially up to four metres in length and more than half a tonne in weight. And this one was really big. To begin with, she came towards us with evident curiosity, turning on her side so that she could get a good look at us. After a while she started upping her game, twisting and turning with every pass, nodding her head from side to side with every cycle. Leopard seals have an extendable neck like a snake, which allows them to snap out at their penguin prey. She started to pirouette, showing us

Ice diving.

her belly, then her graphite-coloured back, peppered with the spots that give the species its name. Just as I was starting to get used to her, it seemed that she decided to punish me for my confidence, to put me in my place and cement her legend. Now, with every pass she would swim into the camera and flash her teeth at me, mere millimetres away. The gape was remarkable, the teeth even more so. Then she started deliberately blowing bubbles at us, another very dramatic threat display.

CLOSE SHAVE

Faced with this leopard seal, I feel very exposed and vulnerable, utterly ill at ease in what is clearly the seal's world. There is no doubt that she could take one of my fins or limbs and just drag me down into the abyss, and there would be nothing I could do about it. Luckily, I have the camera to concentrate on, thinking more about whether it is in focus and if I'm getting the shot, than about what could happen to us.

Then there's a shout from the boat, 'She's just bitten the Zodiac, things are escalating, get out boys, I repeat, get out of the water.' The message has been received loud and clear. We all swim away from the berg and

come to the surface. Now we feel even more at her mercy.
We're bobbing at the surface, and we can't even see her! With the help
of safety divers and my crew, we're all tugged on board wearing our full
kit. Johnny is the last on, and it's the first time I've heard him sound
really panicked, genuinely frightened he could be gripped by the leg
and tugged down into the icy abyss.

Last word to the whales

The journey was all but over, and the crew had taken to the Zodiac in order
to trawl around the icebergs and do a nice piece to finish off the series.
However, the last word was to go to the wildlife, as it always should.

The vast tail fluke of a humpback whale.

Suddenly, three humpback whales popped up right next to us. And when I say right next to us, that's what I mean. You could have reached out and run your hands down their forty-tonne flanks. The leviathans did circuits around our tiny boat, making us feel very small. One cuff of their vast tail flukes could have flipped us, sending us all to the bottom of the frozen sea. But they didn't. It was as if they were giving us an escort, a glorious finale.

Humpbacks are very special animals. They are the most vocal, social and playful of all of the great whales, their front flippers are the largest appendages, and they have the most beautiful voices. They were also special to my Pole to Pole journey. We could not have asked for a more appropriate animal to guide us home. We first saw them feeding on herring, way up north in the Arctic Circle. Then we had witnessed them breaching just metres from our boat in Alaska, before seeing passionate males battling it out in sunny Hawaii. And now here they were, broadsiding us in the Antarctic.

Our journey had spanned the globe, by plane, boat and car, and these wondrous beasts had been with us every step of the way, undergoing the longest migrations of any mammal. For me, it had been a fourteen-month voyage and the greatest adventure of a lifetime; for the humpback whales, a Deadly way of life. It was a perfect and fitting end to our expedition.

THE TEAM

Graham MacFarlane (camera).

The average Deadly team is five strong, which is about the right amount. Any more and you risk creating too much noise and frightening animals away. Any fewer and each person can end up overloaded with work.

Though I wouldn't admit this to their faces, the most skilful job on Deadly is done by the cameramen. If we're about to be charged by a bear, they need to have one eye on the animal and another on their escape route, while still managing to frame up the shot, keep it in focus and have the exposure set right! Just to keep the cameras going in remote environments is a full-time job. The three main cameramen have all been on big expeditions with me. 'Lucky' Luke was on the team that explored the inside of an extinct volcano in

Nick Allinson (sound), Rachael Kinley (director), Luke Cormack (camera).

Steve with Nick Allinson (sound), Kiri Cashell (researcher) and Johnny Rogers (camera).

Papua New Guinea. Graham is probably the most positive 'can-do' person I have ever met; we were both lowered underneath a helicopter into a croc's nest in Oz. Specialist Simon Enderby is one of the finest underwater shooters in the world and a massive bear of a man who scares even the sharks!

Johnny and soundie Nick are the only two people other than me who have been on Deadly since the very beginning and they have been by my side in my two closest calls: when we swam on scuba face first into a hippo, and when we were confronted with an angry giant crocodile underwater, both in the Okavango Delta. The whole bunch has no equal in the world of wildlife filmmaking and I am very lucky indeed to have them on my team.

Luke Hollands (research), Ruth Harries (director) and Simon Cole (sound).

Mike Kasic (sound), Johnny Rogers (camera), Rowan Musgrave (director) and Kiri Cashell (research).

Sound recording was handled by 'Smiley' Simon, Parker Brown, Rich, Gary and of course Nick. They not only record what I'm saying, but also the many wonderful noises the animals make, as well as managing to get sound underwater, in helicopters, and in rain, snow, hail and even tornadoes! They also do a fabulous job of maintaining morale.

The next job is that of director, who's in charge of things when we're on the road. Deadly shoots are not like directing on most TV programmes. There are no scripts, as we really don't know what is going to happen next, so we have to make it all up as we go

Scott Alexander (series producer), Gary Moore (sound), and Graham MacFarlane (camera).

along. Directors Rowan, Ruth and Rachael have to be resourceful and flexible,

steering proceedings with their own unique genius and making sure we film everything they'll need to edit the programmes once back in the UK.

The hardest workers, though, are without doubt the researchers. Toby, Luke, Amy, Gemma and Kiri are all wildlife experts in their own right and do the leg work of organising the shoots, chatting to scientists and local experts and figuring out how best to spend our time on location. When we're away, they'll be filming second camera, taking stills photos, setting up all the mini-cams, and downloading and logging all the footage. They each do the job of about three people, and after a three-week shoot come home and probably sleep for a fortnight!

Series producer Scott Alexander may look more like a surfer dude, but is actually our big boss, the one pulling the strings and making all the big decisions. It's thanks to him shifting budgets around and sweet-talking those with the money that we got to do cool stuff like nearly get eaten by polar bears. He also directed

Ailton Lara, Rachael Kinley (director), Luke Hollands (researcher), Michael Hutchinson (camera), Nick Allinson (sound), Steve Backshall.

Luke Cormack (camera), Rachael Kinley (director), Toby Nowlan (researcher), Simon Cole (sound).

Luke Hollands (researcher), Ruth Harries (director).

on some of the most important shoots, up in the high Arctic and the frozen south. Last but not least, we couldn't shoot a single frame without production manager Janelle and her team back in the office. They rarely get to come away with us, but instead work away tirelessly back in BBC Bristol. They are the mums and dads of the Deadly family, quietly steering us in the right direction, looking after us all, making sure we don't get into trouble, and checking we've got plasters when we graze our knees!

Steve with Scott Alexander (series producer), Ruth Harries (director), Kiri Cashell (researcher), Nick Allinson (sound).

Ailton Lara, Rachael Kinley (director), Nick Allinson (sound), Mike Hutchinson (camera).

This book is a thank you to all of you and an apology that I've caused you so much stress. I really hope you all enjoyed it too.

Caz, Jo, Amy, Janelle, Donna, Ruth – the Bristol team.

PICTURE CREDITS

(b: bottom; t: top; l: left; r: right; c: centre)

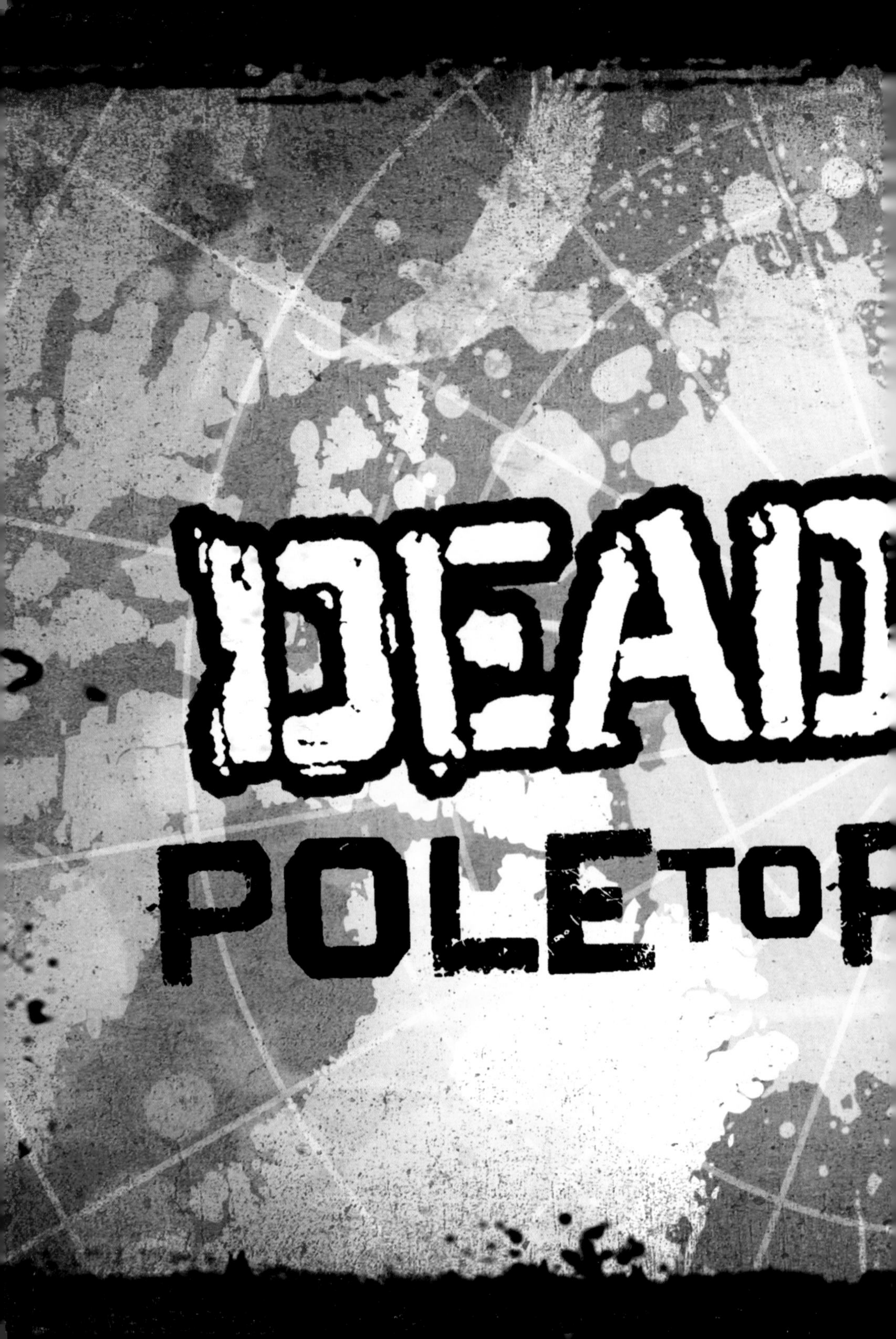